During my research for this book,  a
lot about Harrods, but had not a er
visited me from the States, Harroc it;
however, by the time we arrived it ......

You can imagine my anticipation and apprehension at visiting one of the most famous retail stores where royalties, Hollywood A-list stars and the "who is who" from around the world go shopping.

In my mind, everything in Harrods was made of gold. I even bought a special outfit for the occasion, to ensure I was in sync with the royalties and A-list stars.

I was hoping I could catch a glimpse of Roman Abramovich and some of his billionaire friends or some Saudi prince.

However, instead of Russian oligarch or Middle East Sheikh, what caught my attention was a bus.

I had bought the identical bus for my son from ASDA. It was the same bus in the same packaging.

An odd question popped into my mind when I noticed the bus: Why is it that the same bus, in the same packaging, probably made in the same factory in China, by the same people, was being sold in Harrods for almost three times the price it was sold for in ASDA?

At first it was a mystery to me. But as I walked around Harrods the answer came to me.

ASDA sells toy bus. Harrods sells classy toy bus, even if it is made in the same factory in China.

There is a distinction and that distinction is what this book is about.

The price of a product is not determined by the cost of bringing that product to the marketplace as we are taught in business school, rather by *who is buying, how much they are willing to pay and how the product is sold.*

The reason the same bus, made in the same factory in China is sold in Harrods for almost three times the price it is sold for in ASDA comes down to *who shops at Harrods and how the bus is sold to them.*

For a start, cheapskates like me are not Harrods target market. Harrods know their target market is oil Sheikhs and Russian oligarchs whose focus is not on the product but on the manner in which the product is sold to them.

This is a very important point I will like you to take from this book. Most retailers fail because they ignore this simple but fundamental marketing principle. The majority of retailers do not even know their target market.

They open their stores, stock them with goods and hope that customers will show up simply because they are open for business.

This is a very big mistake!

You first need to decide who you want to sell to and then create a selling environment to attract those types of people.

Harrods have obviously decided who they want to sell to, so they have created a selling environment that appeals to only those types of people.

Their store design and visual merchandise display are created to appeal to their target customers.

Harrods have one of the best store design and visual merchandise display in the retail industry…Period.

I mean that literally, because in my research for this and my other retail books, I researched the best retail stores across the globe.

Most retailers underestimate the relevance of store design and visual merchandise display, to their success.

Your selling environment determines: the customers you attract and the price you can charge.

The retail business is 'showbiz.' So the extent to which you are willing to put up a great performance for your customers, is the extent to which you are going to succeed.

The goal of this book is to teach you the psychology and strategies, behind a beautiful store design and visual merchandise display.

Harrods success is based on three things:

- Good store design
- Beautiful visual merchandise displays
- Effective loss prevention strategies

My aim is to teach you how to replicate a Harrods-like store design and visual merchandise display that enables you sell a made in China toy bus for three times the price it is sold for by other retailers.

This book is not about changing or improving upon what you are already doing; it is about hidden opportunities in your retail business that you have not paid attention to.

It is my guarantee to you that you will easily triple or even quadruple your profit margin in less than 90 days by implementing a third of the information in this book.

About the Author

Romeo Richards is the founder of the Business Education Centre, an institute that shows professional entrepreneurs such as doctors, lawyers, dentists, consultants, trainers, coaches, and security firm owners how to make "7 Figure" in twelve months. He is also the creator of the Business Success Quadrangle Framework and The Blue Ocean Strategy Canvas for: doctors, lawyers, dentists, consultants, retailers, coaches, trainers and security firms.

He has authored eight books on retail profit improvement and is currently writing four additional books on retail store design, visual merchandising, how to market a retail store and how to make profit in retail and the "How to effectively market and manage a professional firm" series for doctors, lawyers, dentists, consultants, trainers, coaches and security firms.

He has authored several White Papers and regularly writes articles on entrepreneur development, retail profit improvement and speak on the same.

How to Increase Retail Sales with Store Design and Visual Merchandise Display

Romeo Richards

www.theprofitexperts.co.uk

+44(0)78 650 49508

romeo@theprofitexperts.co.uk

Dedication

I wrote about vision as your reason for doing anything. I do what I do first and foremost to be an example to my son.

Secondly, to have the ability to help my people shed the curse of poverty.

Alex this book is for you!

Africa this book is in your honour!

Table of Contents

Acknowledgements

My sincere gratitude to Mr. White, John and Michael for editing the book.

Thanks Jen for formatting it and Joseph for managing the entire project.

How to Increase Retail Sales with Store Design and Visual Merchandise Display

How to Design an Attractive but Profitable Store

Romeo Richards

www.theprofitexperts.co.uk

+44(0)78 650 49508

romeo@theprofitexperts.co.uk

Why You Should Read This Book

Why should you read this book when there are literally thousands of retail store design and visual merchandise display books on the market?

For a start, it is the only book on store design and visual merchandise display that talks about the only thing you are interested in: profit.

How can you make profit in your retail store?

You make profit by:

- Increasing sales
- Increasing customer satisfaction
- Increasing staff productivity
- Decreasing shrinkage

In this book, we teach you how to achieve the above objectives through the use of beautiful yet secure store design and attractive visual merchandise display.

No other book on store design and visual merchandise display has ever connected store design and visual merchandise display to those four critical success factors and profit.

There are fundamental principles which underpin good store design and visual merchandise display:

- Customer attraction
- Customer flow
- Persuasion to buy
- Shrinkage management

Your ability to effectively embed these elements into your store design and visual merchandise display strategy will determine your level of success. This book outlines the process for embedding those four elements into your store design and visual merchandise display and sales strategy.

It outlines the best store design and visual merchandise display strategies used by the most successful retailers in the world…Strategies when effectively applied will propel you to unbelievable success.

And here is the icing on the cake, your competitors do not even know most of these strategies. So what you have in your hand is the missing piece of the retail success secret…The ultimate store design blueprint secret.

Introduction

If you are a horror film junkie, you always know when a horror film is about to reach its climax.

If the scene is set in a house, you will notice the camera moving up and down the stairs…then the window flings open…and the moon starts shinning directly into the room…wind begins to blow…the light starts blinking on and off…on and off…and you hear the clock tick…tick…tick…then there is the sound of footsteps in the corridor…then the shadow of the antagonist appears…and then zoom!…without warning the antagonist attacks.

In horror film after horror film, this identical scene plays out all the time. Whether the film is being shot in a house, in the night or day or out in the woods; the costume design and the choreography are always the same.

Why is this always the case with horror and more successful films?

Answer: the directors of horror films understand that the intrigue of the film is not just about the killing or the plot. It is also about the costume design, the sound, the lights, and the background.

When someone goes to watch a horror film, they already know someone is going to die. Therefore the directors understand that the killings no longer scare the audience; it is the events leading to the killing that are intriguing.

What does a horror film have to do with visual merchandise display and what lesson can the retail industry learn from horror films?

The lesson the retail industry can learn from horror films is this: it is not about the merchandise, it is the presentation of the merchandise that matters to the customer.

A good visual merchandise display captures the imagination of targeted audiences just like a good film does. The store is a theatre where customers come to watch a spectacular display of merchandises. If they like the display they will buy, if they don't like the display, they will leave.

The success of great films stems from their ability to cleverly manipulate people's psychology through the brilliant use of words and costume design.

Retailers can do well to emulate the cleverness of the film industry in the presentation of their merchandise if they intent on achieving similar success.

This books aims to show retailers how to choreograph their visual merchandise display and store design strategy to achieve similar success.

The first half of the book deals with the psychology of visual merchandise display and store design. It addresses the questions of understanding your target market and the various strategies for thinking through your visual merchandise display and store design strategy.

Part two deals with the implementation of visual merchandise display. It outlines the best strategies for implementing an effective visual merchandise display strategy.

The store design section deals with the best materials for designing a beautiful store.

Your success as a retailer rests on your ability to create the type of shopping environment that will entice shoppers to visit your store.

The retail environment is changing. These days you are not only competing against other retailers; you are also up against some guy sat in his room selling stuff on the internet.

Consequently, you need to understand that the strategies that worked a few years ago will not work in the new retail environment.

You need a new strategy.

This book contains the new strategies you need to succeed.

Part One
Store Design Blueprint

Chapter One

The Psychology of A Beautiful Store Design

Harrods is one of the more successful retailers in the world. In 2011, in the thick of the global financial crisis; the London based retailer's annual sales were in the region of a billion pounds. When thousands of well-known retail brands were struggling to survive and some forced to close shop.

What is it that makes Harrods more successful than most retail organisations?

Harrods success can be attributed to the following three factors:

- Good store design
- Attractive visual merchandise displays
- Effective loss prevention strategy

The ability to design their store or create visual merchandise displays that incorporate all these elements is one of the determining factors for the success of Harrods and many of the world's most successful retailers.

Harrods' store design is in a class of its own. It is unique, innovative and clever. One important element of their store design is the concept of the stores inside. The store is designed in such a way that as customers move from one department to the next, they get the feeling of moving from one store to another in a shopping centre. Whoever conceived that design concept provided Harrods with a huge competitive advantage over its competitors.

Harrods's visual merchandise displays are as attractive and inviting as displays can get. As customers move from one designer outlet to another; they are met by a completely different display that is indicative of that designer. It is as if the designers themselves went into Harrods to arrange the displays.

Store design and visual merchandise displays need to serve four objectives:

- Attract potential customers as they pass by the store
- Entice those potential customers to enter into the store
- Maintain their interest whilst they are in the store
- Persuade them to buy.

Harrods' ability to effectively utilise these four principles in its store design and visual merchandise displays has been responsible for its phenomenal success.

In his book "Blink", author Malcolm Gladwell introduced the concept of thinking without thinking. "Blink" "the power of thin slicing" and "rapid cognition" is the type of thinking process that occurs in the blink of an eye.

As shoppers walk through a shopping mall of two three hundred stores or a busy high street, they are thin slicing each and every store.

What entices them to choose one store over the other is what Mr. Gladwell alluded to in his first book "Tipping Point"…the little things that make a huge difference. Some of the little things determine whether someone enters your store as opposed to that of your competitor is your store design.

As one walks around Harrods, it is evident that their success does not stem from 'Made in China' products that can be found in stores all over the UK. Their success comes from their ability to apply the principles from "Blink" and the "Tipping Point" to their store design and visual merchandise displays.

Harrods success can be linked to its belief that little things make a big difference:

> Little things like having store associates within easy reach of every customer
>
> Little things like the extraordinary use of mannequins

Harrods success also results from having one of the best store designs and visual merchandising display in the retail industry.

What is Store Design Psychology?

All retailers strive to satisfy every customer that enters their store and give them the kind of service they desire. Offering good customer service and fine quality products are a given in the retail business. But a core element that attracts customers into a retail store is the aesthetics of the store.

The majority of shoppers are more likely to enter a store and purchase when the store has an attractive layout and is convenient for shopping. The key in persuading more shoppers to visit a store lies in it having an attractive store design.

Every retail store has a unique design which entices shoppers into the store. Retail stores are designed to generate an easy and delightful shopping experience. A very important element in retail store design is the psychology that augments the design.

The large windows endowed with eye-catching designs; aisle widths and rack heights are carefully detailed to create a positive feeling which lures shoppers into a store.

All four corners of the store must be viewed and evaluated accurately. The wall colours, signage, checkout counters, racking schemes, displays, and other areas form part of the store layout.

The interior design of a retail store plays a key role in attracting shopper and increasing sales. Proper placement of props such as mannequins and racks help the store to appear more attractive. Creating a theme also helps develop vibes that entice shoppers.

A well designed store makes it convenient and easy for customers to shop. When a shop creates a design concept that matches with the products they are selling, it makes it easier and appealing for the customers to buy.

Furthermore, having a colour scheme that matches the products adds more pleasure for customers to shop. The right colour scheme creates a positive mood for the customer when shopping. For example, a baby clothing store that uses light pastel colours reflects the target market.

The majority of people derive pleasure from shopping in a light and spacious environment. A spacious and clutter-free store is also an advantage for you and your employees.

It becomes easy for your store associates to watch over products and reduce shoplifting. Tables in the central areas, cabinets and shelves towards the back walls create the illusion of a more spacious store.

Apple stores are always packed as customers just love hanging out in their stores. The Early Learning Centre is a children's toy store in the UK. I have been to a few of them and noticed there is not enough space for children to sample toys. You cannot have a toy store that is compact; you lose the potential for sale.

Some retail store designs tend to be excessive. Excessive and unnecessary use of colour and other design elements results in the opposite effect. Instead of enticing shoppers into the store, it repels them.

Therefore, striking the balance between an attractive store that serves as a magnet for shoppers and one that repels them needs an understanding of store design psychology.

Most retailers forget that retailing is about sales and marketing. The most effective marketing strategy a retailer has at his disposal is a well-designed store and attractive merchandise displays.

When there are two or three hundred stores in a shopping centre, the difference between deciding to enter in or pass by a store rests on the design of the store front.

When customers are in a store there needs to be a reason for them to stay longer. The longer they stay, the higher the chances of them buying.

The three main aspects of a store design that keep customers engaged for longer are:

- Designs that enables good customer flow
- An attractive and good lighting system
- Overall atmosphere of the store

Why do people buy?

Why do people buy? We all buy for diverse reasons. The human thought process is complex and irrational. Even though we try to rationalise our actions based upon artificial environmental factors; the reality is, we all do things for the same three reasons:

- Status
- Survival

- Sex

What does everyone want?

In marketing we are taught to believe that individual's wants are different.

This statement is true to an extent but not exactly true. Human psychology has not changed since the dawn of time. The same desire humans had when we lived in caves; we still hold those desires today.

Every prospect, client or customer wants the following three things:

- Result
- Solution
- Relief from something

How these three things manifest themselves in our brain takes the form of the products and services we choose to buy. However, the fundamental principle is this: in the final analysis when customers take out their credit card to buy a product or service, no matter what that product or service is, they are doing so to satisfy all or at least one of the above.

Being aware of that, as you prepare to design your store, here are some questions that should be going through your mind:

1) Which one of the above three are you marketing to satisfy with your store design?
2) Which one of the three are you marketing to satisfy with your shop window display?
3) What emotion are you aiming to trigger?
4) What result should they imagine your store is going to produce for them?

5) What solution should they think your store design would provide?

6) Finally, what pain is the store design going to relieve?

This is not to say that when someone enters your store they will achieve all of those results, your store design just needs to plant the perception of those results in their minds.

But there is a catch. The store designer needs to know the benefit and hidden benefit. It is only when the store designer knows the benefit behind the benefit that they will be able to create a beautiful and attractive store design that captivates your target market.

Figure 1: Think of the benefit behind the benefit in your display

I will use Victoria's Secret as an example. A woman passing by a Victoria Secret store spots sexy lingerie in the shop window; her first thought is: I will look sexy in that or that bra would prop up my cleavage.

But here is the catch, that bra would prop up her cleavage not because she just wants her cleavage propped up but to attract the opposite sex. (I must add a disclaimer that here I am not trying to be sexist I am just using this as an example.)

Therefore as you design your store, your aim should be to match the thinking of the shopper with your store design. Do not design your store to appeal to the beauty of the breast but the outcome that the beautiful breast will result in – the opposite sex!

A major part of store design is being able to analyse shoppers thought process. As was alluded to previously, the human thought process is complex and irrational. The human brain is set up with areas for various functions.

There are three brain types:

- Retile
- Mammal
- Thinker

The problem is these three brains are not integrated. They work separately. The thinking brain is the least dominant of three, which is why our thinking process is in most cases irrational. In the majority of cases, our decisions are based upon triggers from the unconscious.

Remember "Blink"? The power of "thin slices" and "rapid cognition"; this is our predominant thought pattern.

Thin-slicing is a psychological term for the ability to find patterns in events based upon minimal information. It means making rapid decisions with the least amount of information.

When an individual walks through a mall of three hundred stores or on a High Street on Saturday afternoon; his mind races and he thinks at a fast rate. The decision as to which store he enters is made in a blink of an eye.

The merchandise display and store design that catches his attention will win his patronage. Except if he had pre-planned a visit to a particular store; his decisions are based purely upon thin slicing each store as he walks.

Many of our actions, behaviour and thinking originate from the adaptive unconscious, which the majority of us are unaware of.

However, the good news for the retail industry is…other humans are capable of altering those unconscious biases just by tinkering with the little details.

In "The Tipping Point" as I pointed out earlier, Malcolm Gladwell demonstrated how to tinker or social engineer humans to get them to behave in ways we would like them to.

The retail landscape is changing rapidly. Too many choices; disruptions and hoards of information from all directions, either confuse or overwhelm customers.

As the customer walks through a shopping mall, there are gazillion things going through his head. Yours is not the only store in the shopping mall neither is it the only stores design he had seen on that day.

Figure 2: Your window display has to be attractive enough to capture shoppers as they walk pass your shop

There is a cluster of information and stores all around him. Therefore, in order to ensure that your store stands tall above the rest, you need to design it to match his thinking process. That can only be done when you understand store design psychology and use it as a framework for designing your store.

People don't like to be sold but they love to buy, so your store design should sell to them without peddling to them.

The most effective store designs are those that speak directly to the customer's desire for:

- Result
- Solution
- Relief from something

Remember! It is all about:

- Status
- Survival
- Sex

To achieve the above effectively requires you do the following:

- Identify your target market
- Find out what appeals to them
- Incorporate it into your store design

How to apply the principle of store design psychology?

To influence shoppers buying behaviour and design a store that appeals to them demands an in-depth research into your target market's buying habits. This can be done in-house or through an external research agency.

The following steps would assist you implement the psychology of store design effectively:

Step 1:
Conduct, or hire an outside research firm to research into your target market. Using the aims and objectives of your business as a guide...the age, gender, or income group you intend to serve.

Step 2:

Create a store design blueprint tailored to your target market. Focus on colours; types of material; flooring; lighting and fixture arrangement.

Step 3:

Focus the store design on customer flow. This means the aisle width, height and size as well as the location of check-out counters.

Step 4:

Incorporate security and loss prevention into the store design. Pay attention to the location of your entrance and exit, staff areas and warehouse.

A good store design leads to: increased sales, improved staff productivity, reduced shrinkages and increased profit. However, this cannot be done without taking into consideration the psychology of the process.

Things to consider in your store design blueprint:

Display fixtures:

Figure 3: Ensure you consider the types of fixtures you will eventually use when designing your store

Display fixtures are essential components of a retail store design. Consequently, it is essential they are added to the original blueprint.

Lighting system:

Figure 4: Good lighting system enhances the appearance of your store

Lighting plays a crucial role in a retail environment. Lighting has to be a part of the store design blueprint. There needs to be adequate lighting to enhance product appearance.

The placement of the lights should be considered as lights need to be adjusted to accommodate the store layout and climatic conditions.

Fittings:

Figure 5: Fittings need to complement not confuse shoppers

Fittings such as hanging chandelier in the middle of the store, large clock at the rear of the counter and other designs that complement the store's overall appearance need to be also taken into consideration.

Fittings need to be kept to a minimum to avoid confusing the customer. The objective of a store design is to enhance merchandise, not to be points of focus.

Maintaining the ideal design of your store would result in increased sales and brand awareness. Always ensure that you create a lighter aura and a clutter-free store design.

Chapter Two

How To Increase Retail Sales With Attractive Store Design

I have received internet marketing training from the best internet marketers in the world. These are guys who together make billions on the internet each year. Therefore, when attending their training, one would expect them to teach techniques and tricks for making money on the internet.

But whether their training is for a day or a weekend, they spend very little time teaching techniques for using the internet effectively. Instead they focus exclusively on marketing fundamentals. I remember asking one of them during a training section why is it that they do not teach techniques for using the internet effectively. He responded that participants will not be able to effectively use the internet to market their products or services if they do not know basic marketing fundamentals.

Come to think of what he said as I write this book, I believe he was absolutely right. The most successful businesses are not successful because of the industry they are in or because of the product or services they provide; they are successful because they apply simple business and marketing fundamentals.

Apple is a typical example of a business that is not successful because it sells the best products in the world. Its success is based upon the fact that its products function.

Apple's product design is based on three principles:

• Functionality

- Simplicity

- Elegance

Prior to the release of a new Apple product there is the usual hype and buzz around about how good the product is going to be. However, when the product is released the recurrent question that always pops up is what was all the fuss about? There is nothing extraordinary about the product design yet it outsells its competitors. So the question that comes to mind is why is Apple able to outsell its competitors all the time?

Answer: Apple products are functional.

When Apple is about to release a product, its focus is not on how cool the product is going to look but how would it make the life of users easier or even how could it change their lives.

Apple designers go into the head of the average buyer of an Apple product and ask the questions:

Who is the person we are producing this product for?

What work does he do?

Where does he live?

How would this product make his work or home life easy?

What else would he be able to do with this product?

How can this product change his life for the better?

It is only when Apple designers are able to provide answers to the above questions would they embark on the process of designing the product.

Similar thought process goes into the design of cars, whether it is Mercedes-Benz, BMW or Ferrari, their designers ask themselves those question prior to designing their cars.

Mercedes-Benz appeals to a completely different market from BMW or Ferrari. While the average Mercedes-Benz owner might be focused on comfort or luxury, the BMW or Ferrari owner might be focused on speed. Therefore as the designers of these automobile manufacturers sit to design their cars, they concentrate on fulfilling the desires of their target market.

Google arguably one of the most successful businesses of our time has the same web page that it had when it started. Even though it 'Googelise' its logo every day, the design of the webpage remains the same. Which is one of the main reasons it over took other search engines and it continues to dominate the search engine market.

What does the information regarding Apple, Google and automobile manufacturers have to do with retail store design?

Everything!

Retail store design like any other design is subject to similar design principles. In order for a retail store to achieve similar phenomenal success as any other successful business, retail stores have to conform to the same fundamental business principles that make other businesses successful.

For most of this book I am going to use Harrods as an example of a good retail model. The reason for this is that Harrods is one of the most successful retailers in the world.

Therefore, there is no better example to use than one of the most successful retailers in the retail industry. As I searched for the secret behind Harrods' success, I came to the conclusion that the key is its application of the five fundamental business principles:

- Visionary leadership
- Great people

- Good system

- Good marketing system

- Good business model

Take its marketing strategy in its children section for example. When you enter Harrods children, you will first notice play consultants playing with the toys and asking parents and their children to join in the game.

This is basically moving further from just having the children seeing and touching the toys to actually having to play with them to get them emotionally invested in the toys.

Figure 6: Harrods creates the atmosphere for children to sample their toys

After playing with the toy, how many kids will not automatically want to take the toy home with them to continue playing.

In contrast to Harrods, when children and parents enter the Early Learning Centre, it is like a dental suite. The stores is crammed one can hardly breathe. There is nowhere for the children to sample the toys.

Figure 7: Early learning centre stores are like soviet dental suite

Do you see the difference?

Do you see now why it is critical to learn marketing fundamentals before you consider designing your retail store?

One thing you need to learn from the onset is this: the fundamentals of business never change. They remain the same whether it is for the HSBC bank in the city of London or a cleaning business in a dusty New Delhi ghetto. The fundamentals of business are similar to the fundamentals of science or engineering.

The formulas that were used in chemistry since the times of the Roman Empire or the civilization of Egyptian apply to today's chemistry. There might be slight modifications and advancements but the fundamentals remain the same.

The same applies to business. Every successful business has the same five components that make it successful:

- Visionary leadership
- Great people
- Good system

- Good marketing system
- Good business model

The absence of any of the above will cause any business to fail. These are core principles. They are not just something that might be good for a business, they are elements that businesses cannot survive without.

The aim of this chapter is to outline the process of increasing retail sales with attractive store design using those five business success fundaments.

In a book on store design, you will expect techniques and strategies on ways of designing your store to increase sale. However, the best strategies will not work if the person implementing the strategy does not know the reason they are implementing them.

This chapter and the next one would specifically answer the question: why it is important for a retail stores to be designed in a specific way.

I am of the belief that it is only after you have grasped this concept would you be able to derive the maximum benefit from the technique and strategy I will be outlining in subsequent chapters.

However, my aim in this book is not to address the five business fundamentals, I will be dealing with the forth component: a good marketing system. It is my belief that marketing is the most essential of the five business fundamentals.

Conventional wisdom holds that a business cannot make a profit until its third year of operation and we have all bought into that lie. I am here to tell you that, this belief is completely false.

A retail store can begin to make profit from its first month of operation if it applied the principles written in this book. The application of those five core elements is a insurance against any retail business failure.

Understanding how to increase retail sales is very crucial for the success of any retail business and more so now with the increasing failure of many retail businesses.

Background

Lingerie specialist La Senza went into administration in the first week of 2012. It is amongst some 183 UK retailers including: Barratts, Clinton Cards, Habitat, HMV, Focus DIY, JJB Sports, Jane Norman, Mothercare, Oddbins, TJ Hughes and Thorntons that got into trouble in 2011. This is in addition to the thousands of retailers that went bust without making the headlines.

The British Prime Minister alarmed by the prospects of many UK town centres turning into ghost towns, appointed a committee headed by UK retail guru, Mary Portas, to look into why the UK High Street was at risk of extinction.

Her report concluded that the main reason for the demise of the High Street was:

"High Streets have reached 'crisis point' with the rise of super-malls, out-of-town supermarkets and internet shopping".

This follows another report by Colliers CRE which highlighted the "downward spiral and degenerating or failing" of the UK High Street.

As I write this book, the Australian government has also commissioned a report into the future of the Australian retail industry.

So why is the retail industry facing such difficulty even though literally no one can survive without visiting a retail store?

The answer to this question is simple:

The retail industry is the only industry where increased sales area is the key performance indicator.

A large part of this chapter was written as a White Paper on Boxing Day (2011), which is the day when most retailers start their biggest sales of the year. The irony is even though they make their biggest sales on that day, the large majority of retail stores did not make a single red penny in profit.

How can a business expect to make a profit from discounting products at 50% or 70%? Retail profit is an average of 3%. Even the most profitable retailers make between 3 and 5% profit.

The large majority of retailers make a profit margin of between 1.5–3%. Therefore, if a retailer is making a 3% profit margin and is discounting his merchandise by 50%, how much profit will he be making?

I am aware that it might sound contradictory that I am writing a chapter on how to increase retail sales with attractive store design yet seem to be criticising the concept of increasing sales.

I would like to clarify the fact that I am not critical of the concept of increasing sales, increased sales must also simultaneously result in increased profit.

To increase sales without simultaneously increasing profit is a wasted opportunity.

Therefore, my aim in this chapter is to show you how to increase sales while increasing profit.

How to increase retail sale and profit simultaneously

The 18th century business environment was about speed. The 19th century business environment was about quality. The 21st century business environment is about two things:

- Value
- Total customer experience

What is value?

Value is a quantifiable benefit between both parties involved in a transaction. The key phrase here is: quantifiable benefit. Value has to be sensory specific.

I will further nail down the definition of value with quotes from renowned business experts starting with the Oracle of Omaha, Warren Buffett:

> *"Price is what you pay. Value is what you get."*

Value according to Ron Baker is the amount a customer is willing to pay for a product or service.

> *"Too many people think only of their own profit. But a business opportunity seldom knocks on the door of self-centred people. No customer ever goes to a store merely to please the storekeeper."* Kazuo Inamori, founder of KYOCERA Corp.

> *"The successful producer of an article sells it for more than it cost him to make, and that's his profit. But the customer buys it only because it is worth more to him than he pays for it, and that's his profit. No one can long make a profit producing anything unless the customer makes a profit using it."* Samuel B. Pettengill.

The above quotations by prominent business thinkers were introduced to emphasise the point that for a product or service to be considered valuable, it has to benefit both you and your customers.

What is total customer experience?

Marcus Buckingham in his book "The One Thing You Need to know" wrote that when he interviewed Sir Terry Leahy the man who propelled Tesco into a global brand, he asked him: how he turned Tesco from a UK retailer to the fourth biggest retailer in the world.

Sir Terry told him that when he took over Tesco, the first thing he did was to ask and answer the question: who do we serve?

This question is classic marketing 101: know thy customer.

When they established who they were going to serve, he put in place mechanisms for ensuring they serve their preferred customer. One of those mechanisms they put in place was to increase the numbers of checkout counters in each Tesco store.

When asked why he focused on the checkout counters, he replied with something to the tune of; part of good customer service was to show respect for your customer and what better way of showing respect for someone than showing respect for their time.

21st century retail success therefore, would not be just about the quality of the products you sell or the price you sell them for, but the total customer experience when they visit your store. Total customer experience is your entire package:

- The quality of your products
- The price of your products
- The way your staff interact with the customers
- The way the merchandises are displayed

• Your store design

Below is a list of good customer service quotes that I hope will help you in your journey towards providing total customer experience.

"Do what you do so well that they will want to see it again and bring their friends". Walt Disney.

"It's our job every day to make every important aspect of the customer experience a little bit better." Jeff Bezos, founder of Amazon.

"Your most unhappy customers are your greatest source of learning." Bill Gates, founder of Microsoft.

"There is only one boss. The customer and he can fire everybody in the company from the chairman on down, simply by spending his money somewhere else". Sam Walton, founder of Wal-Mart, the world's largest retailer.

"Customers do you a favour by choosing to do business with you. You aren't doing them a favour by serving them." Mark Sanborn

"If you're not serving the Customer, you'd better be serving someone who is." Jan Carlzon, former president of SAS Airlines

"People will forget what you said. People will forget what you did. But people will never forget how you made them feel." Maya Angelou

"If your business cannot pledge 100% Satisfaction Guaranteed or your money back something is broken. Fix it…No customer walks into your business, gives you money and then says, Dissatisfy me, please. Aim for 100% customer satisfaction…Delivering good customer service is business common sense. Your job is to make it common practice". Bill Quiseng

Retail success fundamentals

In addition to "Level five" leadership and good loss prevention strategy, the key components that have been responsible for the success of a few retail organisations are the following:

- Understanding of their target market
- Trained staff
- Skilled sales staff
- Product knowledge
- Great customer service provision
- Understanding of Their Target Market

I visited Harrods for research about this book and my book on visual merchandise display, Harrods, as previously stated is the Mecca of retailing. Royalty, A-list celebrities and the 'who's who' from around the world fly into London just to shop at Harrods.

You can now imagine my anticipation when I visited Harrods. In my mind everything in Harrods was made of gold. I was disappointed, when I noticed a toy bus I had purchased for my son from ASDA, was also being sold in Harrods.

It was exactly the same toy bus, in exactly the same packaging as the toy in ASDA.

A question popped into my mind, why is it that exactly the same bus, probably manufactured in exactly the same factory in China, is sold in Harrods for twice the price that it is sold for in ASDA?

The answer is decisively simple – ASDA sells a 'toy bus', however, Harrods sells a 'classy toy bus'.

There is a difference.

This is marketing 101: people buy emotionally but justify their decision logically.

Customers who shop at Harrods do not shop there to buy Harrods' products; they shop at Harrods to buy elegance and class. Harrods sells them class even if it is 'Made in China'.

How does Harrods pull this off?

They achieve it with the combination of an elegant store design and attractive visual merchandising displays.

When you move from one department to the next in Harrods, it is like moving from one store to another. Their ability to use their store design to create the illusion of differentiation is one of the keys to Harrods' success.

Harrods understand their customers; they know what their customers desire so they design their store and display their products to satisfy the desire of their customers.

> Tesco serves the ordinary Joe Bloke.
>
> Wal-Mart serves the person who lives: pay check to pay check.
>
> The Body Shop serves the ethical consumer.
>
> Waitrose and Holland & Barrett serve the consumer who wants to live longer.

Ann Summers took merchandise once hidden in secret 'adult' shops; made them chic and took them to the High Street. They made a taboo subject acceptable to the mainstream.

If I was to take my partner shopping at John Lewis, she would probably phone my mother to inform her that I was having a nervous breakdown. She would not want to be caught dead in a John Lewis' outfit. She describes John Lewis' clothing department as a

Bridget Jones museum where they store a collection of Bridget Jones costumes.

However, John Lewis continues to increase profits year on year because John Lewis understands their target market.

Someone like my significant other might not want to be caught dead in John Lewis' outfit, but there are people in the UK, who love Bridget Jones' memorabilia, these people are John Lewis' target market, so John Lewis caters to them.

The most successful retailers understand their target market and show their understanding of their target market through their store design and visual merchandising displays.

On Christmas Eve, I had not done my grocery shopping and was dreading the prospect of entering a supermarket, knowing how packed they were going to be. But as I drove past my local Lidl store, I noticed it was empty. I rushed in and completed my shopping.

As I drove back home a question came to my mind; why is it that even on this day when most supermarkets are typically jam packed was Lidl empty?

The answer is: Lidl does not have a target market. One of their biggest sins was making the decision to force customers to pay for carrier bags. Marks & Spencer can afford to do that because they appeal to a different class of customers.

In Tesco and ASDA, customers who are environmentally conscious have the option of paying for carrier bags. However, those who do not want to pay for carrier bags also have the option of getting free bags.

This is because Tesco and ASDA understand their customers. Lidl's senior management, on the other hand, believed that having implemented a similar strategy in Europe, they could do the same in the UK. If the Brits do not like it, tough! Well, the Brits had shown their displeasure with their feet.

I have used the above examples to demonstrate that success or failure in retail is the result of the strategies every retailer adopts. Those retailers who understand their target market and cater to them will continue to move from success to greater success. Those who roll the dice and hope that customers show up are the ones who will struggle or go into administration.

I hate to be the one breaking this type of news to the retail industry but I guess someone will have to do it: the internet is not going away. This means that retailers are not only competing with one another, they are also competing with factory owners in China whose names they have never heard. Shoppers are now ordering directly from warehouses and distributors, for example an individual can log on to eBay and order a pallet load of goods.

Here is the good news: the majority of people still prefer to shop from physical retail outlets. The question for you is this: how do you ensure that shoppers are attracted to your store?

It can be done by designing your store to take into account their buying habits.

Trained Staff

A friend of mine is a manager at Tesco. He knows the profit margin on each and every product in his store. Why does knowing the profit margins matter for his products?

There are numbers of reasons. Firstly business is about making profit and secondly it highlights the significance of "training" to retail success.

As a manager at Tesco, my friend receives periodic training on every aspect of running a retail business. Little wonder Tesco is the second most profitable retailer in the world and the third most profitable business in the UK.

Tesco, like most successful retailers, understand the significance of staff training to the success of their business. Subsequently, they ensure their staff are constantly trained.

> *It never ceases to amaze me how an individual will open a retail store worth millions of pounds only to have the store managed by someone they are unwilling to spend a few hundred pounds to train.*

The two common excuses retailers give for not training their staff are:

- It is expensive
- Absentee cover

I'm probably the only person who doesn't get it, just imagine this scenario:

Someone, somewhere, is leaving his multi-million pound retail store in the hands of an individual and he says it is too expensive to spend a few hundred pounds to provide that person with the requisite training to manage his store well; can you imagine that?

What am I missing?!

Sales Training

According to a survey commissioned by Blue Martini Software; retailers could be losing up to 85 billion pounds per year as a result of inadequate staff training. The survey revealed that 84% of potential customers who left stores without buying said they were going to buy from another retailer.

This means that the store they entered was unable to sell them on yes, so they sold them on no.

As many as 95% of retail employees have never received any form of sales and marketing training. As a result of their inability to sell, most retail staff just stand by as shoppers examine merchandise and cross their fingers hoping they will decide to buy.

Worst of all are the ones who keep asking the same stupid question for which they know exactly the answer they are going to get: "can I help you?"

"No I am just looking"

Retailing is about selling. This means that anyone in retail should at the very least be given basic sales training.

If retailing is about selling and 95% of retail staff have never received any form of sales training, surely there is a linear relationship between sales training and retail success.

It is like a medical doctor who has never been to medical school, how many people in this world would want an untrained doctor to treat them?

Product Knowledge

Covert sting operations, conducted by 'Which?' the consumer organisation, in 2011, revealed that many retail employees lacked knowledge of the products they sold. Just 8 out of the 154 stores investigated, scored an excellent mark. No well-known High Street brand was amongst those eight.

Surprised?

Maybe not.

In this information age where consumers have access to vast amounts of information one would expect retailers to realise the importance of product knowledge for their staff.

Nowadays, many shoppers search on the internet for products prior to stepping foot in a shop. They read information such as product specification, where to get the best deal and customer reviews. They visit shops to basically clarify what they have already read. If the store staff are unable to answer their questions, there is no chance that they will be able to sell to them.

Here is the secret, despite the fact that people conduct research on the internet, the large majority still don't trust information found on the internet. That is why books are still highly rated even though the information in most books can be found online.

People still trust other people and prefer to interact with people. This is one reason why despite the internet, bricks and mortar retailing will survive. However, there is a new dynamic and retailers need to understand this.

The consumer of today is better informed than the consumer of ten or twenty years ago. Consequently, today's retail staff need to be better informed than the retail staff of ten or twenty years ago.

One cannot navigate the 21st century with a 19th century skill set; it will not work.

Richer Sounds has been featured in the Guinness Book of Records for the past 20 years as having the highest sales per square foot of any retailer in the world.

Coincidentally, they continue to top the 'Which?' survey for excellent customer service and product knowledge.

Good Customer Service Provision

These days, the only reason I visit my local PC World store is to buy ink for my printer. This is due to the fact that it is the only retailer in my locality that sells the type of ink cartridge suitable for my printer.

Every time I enter a PC World store, I encounter a similar level of service. I am always forced to queue up for a long time at the checkout, waiting for staff to serve me. Even when the store is empty I have to wait to be served, whilst there will be a group of staff chatting a few metres away from the vacant checkout.

PC World and her sister company Curry's are struggling and their management wonder why?

I am sure if they were to go bust the CEO would blame harsh trading conditions. The fact that his store ranks at the bottom of many customer satisfaction surveys would not be seen as a factor in their demise.

In this "Long Tail" retail environment where consumers are constantly presented with endless choices, one would think that retailers, especially High Street retailers would realise the importance of excellent customer service and try to instil it as a fundamental part of their business strategy.

Thirty to 40% of people will buy solely on price. The majority 70% of people will buy on quality and convenience. Even though the retail industry is in crisis, the luxury sector of the industry is still growing strong. This is because no matter what the economic situation is people still shop. The only question is where will they shop.

Luxury retailers understand this fact and train their staff in excellent customer service.

I have noticed in my local ASDA that when staff are asked for information, they do not just point; they take customers to the location and ask them what else they can do for them.

People go to restaurants where the food is terrible but never complain because of the attitude of the staff. However, if it was the other way around, the food tasted great but the service sucked, they are highly unlikely to return to that restaurant.

Good customer service is a key component to the success of many of the most successful retailers whilst bad customer service has been one of the major contributing factors for the failure of many retail ventures.

This is a book about store design, I am sure you would expect me to provide you with tips about designing the physical aspect of your store. So why does it seem as though I am going on about subjects that do not seem related to store design?

The answer is this: store design is about marketing. Remember a business needs five components to succeed:

- Visionary leadership
- Great people
- Good system
- Good marketing system
- Good business model

The life blood of any retail business is its ability to acquire and retain customers. Your success as a retailer will depend on your ability to acquire and retain customers. Your store design is a critical part of your marketing process. Your ability to design your store making use of fundamental business principles will determine your level of success.

One thing you need to understand is, the store design itself is not going to attract customers or increase your sales, your ability to use your store design as a vehicle for the achievement of customer acquisition will be the determining factor.

As stated previously, the likes of Google, Facebook and all of the successful internet entrepreneurs are not successful because of their ability to use the internet better than the rest of us. They are successful because of their ability to effectively use the internet as a tool through which they can apply fundamental business principles.

> In Value Migration, Adrian Slywotzky stated that "A business (model) design is the totality of how a company selects its customers, defines and differentiates its offerings (or responses), defines the tasks it will perform itself and those it will outsource; configures its resources; goes to market; creates utility for customers and captures profits. It is the entire system for delivering utility to customers and earning a profit from that activity".

In their paper "while the term 'business model' is often used these days, it is seldom defined explicitly." Chesbrough and Rosenbloom point out that there are six specific functions of a business model:

- Articulate the value proposition – the value created to users by using the product.
- Identify the market segment – to whom and for what purpose is the product useful; specify how revenue is generated by the firm.
- Define the value chain – the sequence of activities and information required to allow a company to design, produce, market, deliver and support its product or service.
- Estimate the cost structure and profit potential – using the value chain and value proposition identified.

- Describe the position of the firm with the value network – link suppliers, customers, counterparts and competitors.

- Formulate the competitive strategy – how will you gain and hold your competitive advantage over competitors or potential new entrants.

Joan Magretta wrote in the Harvard Business Review in May 2002: *"A good business model answers Peter Drucker's age-old questions: "Who is the customer?" And "what does the customer value?" It also answers the fundamental questions every manager must ask: How do we make money in this business? What is the underlying economic logic that explains how we can deliver value to customers at an appropriate cost"?*

Your retail store is first and foremost a business and like any business it is dependent on your marketing process – your ability to acquire and retain customers; the extent to which you are capable of marketing your retail store with an attractive store design that is focused on providing value and total customer experience, will be the extent to which you are going to succeed.

Incidentally while writing this chapter; I took a break to relax. I switched on the television. BBC Click was on. The program was about new types of buildings that respond to the movement of people.

Just like the new great buildings that are being constructed to generate energy automatically, the building will be capable of changing in relation to the movement of people. Even a chair will adjust itself to suit the shape of the person sitting on it.

In short, buildings of the future are going to be designed on functionality. The question that this brings to mind is: How functional is your retail store?

Is your store designed for the customers of two decades ago or is it designed for customers of the next two decades?

Let me provide you a few tips on how to design a retail store that results in increased sales:

Step 1:
Identify your target market.

Step 2:
Find out what factors influence their buying behaviour.

Step 3:
Focus your store design exclusively on satisfying the desires and buying behaviours of your target market.

Step 4:
Choose colour schemes, fixtures, fittings, display space, location of cashier counter, location of customer services desk, shelf height, in accordance with the findings made in your target market research.

Step 5:
Incorporate the security of your merchandise into your store design. This is the most important aspect of the store design as stores need to be designed in such a way that they design-out crime. (Whether it is employee theft or shoplifting; a well-designed store can effectively design out crime.)

Step 6:
Take the effective use of technology into account when designing your store. Whether it is a POS, CCTV or EBR system they all need to be included in the design blueprint. A good POS system can rapidly increase sales by reducing queues. CCTV and EBR systems reduce crime whether shoplifting or employee theft.

Chapter Three

How to Increase Retail Sales With Brand Image Selling

There is more to retailing than merchandise and selling. It is also about your customers' perception of your brand and what it represents. Their perception and the connection they make with your brand and what it represents is the most important component of your marketing strategy.

Retail business is like showbiz. It is all about image, brand and style. Many people choose to work in a particular business, not because of the financial reward they hope to gain, but the value the business represents.

Most people associate The Body Shop with ethics.

Harrods is perceived as elegant and classy.

Victoria's Secret is the lovers' choice for lingerie.

Customers who shop at The Body Shop do so largely because their products are not tested on animals. They also feel that by purchasing The Body Shop products they are swaying their conscience.

Harrods markets itself as an elegant store that attracts classy people. Royalties the world over, Hollywood 'A' list stars and the 'who is who' in the world go to London specifically to shop at Harrods, all because it has created an image of elegance.

Victoria's Secret is the preferred choice for ladies shopping for lingerie for that special occasion. In the minds of most of them, Victoria's Secret has come to represent love. When women want to go on a special date or when they want to surprise their significant other, they shop for their special bedroom lingerie at Victoria's Secret. Wearing lingerie from Victoria's Secret gives them confidence.

These retailers have carved a place in the hearts of shoppers by getting them to link their brand with their image. The image cultivated by those brands has been responsible for their phenomenal success in the retail industry.

Image selling is vital for the success of any retail venture, without it most retail businesses struggle. Image selling is a very effective sales strategy and used properly, it can make the selling process very easy.

The crux of image selling is twofold:

- The image that the customer wants to portray by purchasing your merchandise
- The image that the customer already knows that your store represents

A person willing to spend a quarter of a million pounds to buy a Ferrari is not doing so simply because he wants to drive a fast car. He chose to buy a Ferrari because of the prestige associated with owning a Ferrari.

Every person deep down wants recognition and the appreciation of others. Shrewd marketers tap into the human desire for recognition and craft their marketing messages to fulfil that desire.

In his book "Breakthrough Advertising" Eugene Schwartz describes this human behaviour as identification. He defined identification as:

"the desire of a person to act a certain role in their lives and to define himself to the world around him—to express the qualities within himself that he values and the position he has attained. All products may benefit from the power to define. But in particular,

when you have a product that does the same job as competing products, and is so priced that price is no longer a factor then expect choice will almost overwhelmingly depend on the difference in role that your product offers him".

I once watched an interview with a Ferrari executive. He let it be known that when you drive a Ferrari, you drive a dream.

This statement is so true.

Most men who are into cars view Ferrari as the ultimate driving machine. Although it is not the most expensive car in the world, driving a Ferrari is like a dream come true for many people.

As you design your store you need to be considering the roles and characteristics you want your customers to associate it with. Whatever role and characteristic you choose must be one they already possess in their head. You cannot invent a role or characteristic from thin air.

Remember? Driving a Ferrari is driving a dream.

Going into your retail store is what...Complete the sentence.

I attended a business start-up event in London and met a few retail businesses. When I interviewed the retailers at the stands about what made their products different from those of the other retailers in the arena, not a single one could tell me any differentiating factor. They all said their products were made specifically for the consumer et cetera, et cetera.

I kept priming them to see if at least one could come up with anything that was closely relate to the benefit the customer will derive from purchasing their products. Not a single one was able to come up with the benefit of their products to their customers.

A prerequisite for success in the retail industry or in any business for that matter is the ability to differentiate your business from that of the competition.

The second aspect of image selling is the association you want your customers to have with your brand.

Image selling is the ability to market an idea that people cling to, that which in the end creates a positive perception in their mind about your brand.

Certain brands are associated with ethics, healthy lifestyle, elegance, class, low quality, safety, innocence or quality.

However, to sell an image effectively, the image has to be implanted in the minds of your customers from the start of your business.

Certain retail organisations have been trying to flaunt their Green credentials by selling carrier bags. Although they might be honestly doing it for environmental reasons, the fact that they had not done it from their formative stages leads most people to think they are just doing it as an excuse to increase their profit margin.

Europe based supermarkets such as ALDI and LiDL operating in the UK and US charge for carrier bags. However, they have been doing so from the start of their operations in those countries, even though other retailers give carrier bags for free. Therefore, no one will accuse them of charging for carrier bags to increase profit.

The image your retail organisation projects could be that of the philosophy of the founder. Your organisation could represent *fun, love or passion for life.*

It really does not matter what image you choose to project. What is important is your brand is associated with something. To maintain that image, your store and entire work environment should reflect that image.

For example, if the image you want to project is that of a fun-loving organisation, your store colours should be bright and it should be designed to be cheery.

If you want to project the image of an environmentally conscious organisation; then your store colour should be green and it should be designed so that all of your fixtures are made from recyclable materials.

However, your brand image is not just your logo, colour or store design. It is also your brand promise. It is what customers can expect when they interact with your brand. A good brand image is part and parcel of the retail success secret of successful retailers and is a very effective marketing tool utilised with laser accuracy by those retailers.

Although image is intangible; it is more valuable than the products in your store.

Just the Logo of multinational corporations such as Coca Cola, Nike, Google and Apple carry a value many times that of some developing countries. Those multinationals spare no effort because they know that brand sells the products not the other way round.

Nike represents hero

Timberland represents adventure

Rolex represents luxury

Why is image and branding so important for store design?

Branding and image is important because they are the information upon which the store design blueprint is based. When customers enter your store, they need to be able to connect to your brand image inside the store.

Your brand image is an implicit promise to your customers about who you are and what you represent, consequently it is essential that you jealously protect and promote your image.

Store design fundamentals

"So with any other mail order ad which has long continued. Every feature, every word and picture teaches advertising at its best. You may not like them. You may say they are unattractive, crowded, hard to read — anything you will. But the test of results has proved those ads the best salesman those lines have yet discovered. And they certainly pay" (Claude C. Hopkins – Scientific Advertising).

The above summarises the concept of creating a marketing design. Most retailers have not connected their store design with their marketing strategies so they leave the design of the store to store fitters with no knowledge about marketing or advertising.

As I previously pointed out the difference between someone passing by your store in a busy shopping centre and entering your store, rests upon your store design.

Most designers equate beauty with good design. The aim of a marketing design is not to impress customers with beauty. It is to enhance your marketing message. Some marketing designs don't work because those creating the design do not understand the fundamentals of marketing design.

Most designers think that it is about adding fancy images to a design to make it look fanciful. Fanciful designs are good for comics and children's' books. In the marketing world it is about the message.

Every component of the design has to serve the purpose of enhancing the core marketing message, not distract from it.

The one thing that should be uppermost in your mind when it comes to marketing design is simplicity. Most Apple products are not the best designed products in the world. However, they outsell all products in their niche.

Why, because Apple focuses on *simplicity, elegance and functionality.*

Their products are functional and elegant.

Google website is one of the top five high traffic websites in the world. Yet the Google home page is just the Google logo, and a few tabs at the top.

Look at ads in the top selling newspapers and magazines. You will notice that they are mostly in black and white and most of them have no images, only essential information relating to the product or service.

When the London 2012 logo was unveiled, no one except the designers seemed to know what they had designed. Some people described it as a child's drawing. Some say it symbolised an angry reaction.

It was call various things, but a reference to the Olympics. The chairman of the London organising Olympic committee had to go on television to explain to the British public what the logo meant.

When a logo is designed for an event as popular as the Olympics and no one understands the design, there is a serious design fault.

Figure 8: London 2012 Olympic logo confused everyone

This is a lesson for you. Pay attention. As you create your store design you need to ensure that the design is clearly understood by your target market and that it appeals to them.

The goal of your store design has to be:

- Simplicity
- Functionality
- Clarity

Why do most advertising fail?

"Some ads are planned and written with some utterly wrong conception. They are written to please the seller. The interests of the buyer are forgotten. But one can never sell goods profitably, in person or in print, when that attitude exists" (Claude C. Hopkins – Scientific Advertising).

Although store design is advertisement, many store designs fail to attract customers for the same reasons that many advertisements fail to attract customers' attention.

Look at your current store design and ask yourself the following questions:

- Was it designed with the customer in mind?
- Does your store fit with your customer avatar?

- Did you take into account your competition?
- Is your store design simple, functional and clear?
- Does your store design represent your core message?

If you cannot answer all the above questions in the affirmative, you will want to reconsider your current store design.

How to design a store that represents your brand image

The following steps are effective for creating your image:

Step 1:

Identify the image you want to be associated with. It can either be the philosophy of the founder or the organisation as a whole. It first needs to be identified along with the story of why you want to be associated with that particular image.

Step 2:

Communicate that image to your store designer in order for it to be incorporated into the store design blueprint.

Step 3:

Design your store to reflect that image. Every fixture, lighting and decor in the store needs to be congruent with that image.

Step 4:

Ensure all store assistants are well briefed and up to speed on your brand image. Their uniforms, actions and interaction with customers need to reflect your projected image.

The main point to remember here is that as powerful as image selling is, it is a process. It is not an event. It is a process that needs to be consciously built into your marketing strategy and plan from your formative stages.

What is Brand Image?

The most successful retailers have carved out an image that the buying public can easily associate them with.

How to Market Your Brand Image?

Steps for Marketing Your Brand Image

The following steps will help you to effectively market your image:

Step 1:

Identify your desired brand image. You need to have a mission and value statement that articulates what you stand for. It must also contain information about why you stand for that.

Step 2:

Ensure your store designers fully understand the image you want to project to your customers in order for every aspect of it to be incorporated into your store design blueprint.

Step 3:

Ensure your store is designed in congruence with your desired image.

Step 4:

Ensure all employees within your organisation are aware of your brand image and adhere to it in every aspect of their job.

Your brand image is the most valuable asset in your retail organisation, it is an intangible asset. A good image can make you successful. A negative image will cause you to fail, so build and guard your image and ensure that the message of your image is communicated to your store designers.

Chapter Four

Designing Store For Increase Customer Flow

In chapter one, I mentioned two retailers from different spectrum of the retail success continuum: Harrods one of the most successful retailers in the world and Early Learning Centre a struggling UK retailer.

They both sell children's toys.

In Harrods children are able to play with the toys in the store strategically stimulating an attachment to the toys that results in them pressurising their parents to buy it for them.

While the Early Learning Centre has a Soviet style dental suite store where children cannot even breathe or walk around without stepping on each other's toes and parents have to stay outside of the store when their children are inside.

Increasing retail sales requires four core elements

- Attracting customers as they pass by the store
- Enticing them to enter the store
- Retaining them longer in the store
- Persuading them to buy

There is not a single one of these four core elements that one would stand out as a single factor that on its own can result in increased sales. However, if it is a case of being forced to choose one from four, I will say retaining customers in the store would be the most important of the four. This is because the longer customers stay in the store, more likely they are to buy.

To hold customers in your store for a long time, they need to be able to move freely within the store without any form of hindrance. A retail store has three basic design components:

1) Selling area

2) Services area

3) Circulation area

The extent to which these areas are effectively utilised, especially the selling area will have an effect on the success of the retailer.

Shopping is a favoured pastime for many people. For a great many people shopping is a necessity. However, in a majority of the cases, recreational shopping is more prevalent than shopping out of necessity. Visit any city centre at the weekend and you will notice the High Street jam packed with shoppers. Despite the hoard of people in the city centre, as you walk around, you will notice some packed and empty stores.

Have you ever wondered why this is the case?

The reason for this is that for most people the act of going to shopping is an event. Those who buy for recreational purposes do not go shopping just to buy things. They love the experience. There might be ten thousand people in the city centre on a particular day, but each one of them has a personal reason for being in the city.

The stores that attract the most customers are those that appeal to the reasons for those people being in the city centre. 21st century retailing is not about buying and selling, it is also about the experience that customers have in the process; it is about the atmosphere in the store and how comfortable customers feel in it.

Starbucks sells coffee like many other coffee shops, yet people prefer Starbucks to other coffee shops. Starbucks does not sell some types of technologically advanced coffee that is proven to give long life, yet customers prefer Starbucks over other Cafes.

This is due to the fact that Starbucks creates an environment in which customers feel relaxed and comfortable. When customers feel this way they are more inclined to purchase more coffee. A similar principle applies to your retail store. It must be a place where customers will not only come to buy what they need but also somewhere that they like to relax.

An Apple store in a shopping centre is always full of people. Even in the middle of the day when most retail stores are empty, Apple stores are buzzing with people. The reason for that, Apple stores are cool places to be.

Many people make buying decisions in the store after they have had the time to browse the merchandises. You want your customers spending their time buying, and not waste time navigating clutter.

The goal of any retail store is to attract customers and then persuade them to buy. Good advertising and promotion works to bring customers into the store. But when they are in the store, their decision to buy could be down to the layout and design. Both play a huge role in how customers rate their experiences, whether they buy and if they return or recommend the store to others.

Think about the experience you want to create for customers who enter your store. Picture the type of store design that would make it possible for customers to move from the front to the rear of the store browsing products and how they will go to the checkout counter without encountering obstacles.

Another important element in customer flow is the interaction of your store's sales assistants with customers:

When customers enter your store, how are they greeted?

When they need help, are store associates ready to assist them?

Are they trained to provide answers to the costumers' questions?

I know a sports retailer in the UK that spends millions advertising in prime locations all around the country. However, when customers visit their stores, there are never enough store associates to serve them and when they have a question; the store associates haven't a clue.

How do you display high-value and impulse items?

Do you strategically locate high-value and impulse products?

Take some time to strategically locate high ticket items. It will determine your level of sales of those items. One objective of your store design should be to create a space where customers and sales associates can move freely, maximize space and make the most of your product exposure.

What is customer flow?

Customer flow in a retail environment refers to the manner in which customers move from the point of entry into the store until they leave the store. Customer flow refers to the ease with which customers walk through the aisles; many ways in which they gain access to products, sample products, have their questions answered and ease with which they pay for products and exit the store.

A good customer flow system should respond to customer's choice. The customer should have visible options. These ought to include easy access to products and customer service that results in positive impression of your store.

In a retail environment where the entire operation depends on various actors and factors, customer flow doesn't just happen. It must be purposely created as a part of your store design blueprint; managed and continuously improved to take into account the changing retail environment.

Store design plays a key part in relation to customer flow because the design of the store facilitates easy movement of your customers from end to end.

Your store is a stage for your brand; a display case for your products and an exceptional three-dimensional experience for your customers. The design, style and finish of your store will have a powerful, lasting impact on customer loyalty and purchasing decisions.

Aisle signage and shelf labelling form another part of your customer flow plan. Throughout the store signage and labelling should be set to enable customers locate products easily and familiarise themselves with the store layout.

You might want to consider seasonal themes. In summer you can create tropical scenery to lure customers to an area in the store where they can view related products and so on.

What are the various types of store design?

Listed below are the three basic types of store designs that encourage customer flow:

Free flow design

The Free flow design system allows products to be arranged throughout the store. Use racks and shelves that enable customers to browse freely with store associates on hand and ready to provide assistance when necessary.

A free flow store design is mainly used in boutiques, clothing, jewellery, and specialty stores. The cons of this design is: if display racks and products are not well arranged the store can appear cluttered and difficult for customers to navigate.

Grid pattern design

The Grid pattern design is usually used by drugstores, supermarkets and superstores. Mostly used in a rigid retail environment that offers less flexibility and encourages customers to search for items on their own.

But a grid pattern layout requires multiple rows filled with a variety of products throughout the store. High ticket items are displayed in high traffic locations and end caps so the customer can't help but notice them.

Such locations also support impulse buying. With a Grid pattern design customers are only able to familiarise themselves with the store layout and location of products after repeated visits.

Spine design

The spine design contains elements of the free flow and grid pattern store design. It is the third most commonly used retail store design strategy. It has a single long main aisle that goes from the entrance of the store to the back of the store. With the spine design, products can be displayed on both sides of the aisle using either the free flow or grid layout or a combination of the two. This design is mostly favoured by department stores because of the different range of products they display.

How to use store design to increase customer flow

A research into customer flow in the UK revealed that 75% of customers only saw a maximum of 25% of products on display in a retail store.

Just pause and think for a moment!

What will happen to your sales if your customers saw at a glance, all of the products on display in your store.

Your objective should be to design your store in such a way that it leads customers around the store. Furthermore, the aim has to be to create a design that ensures they are purposefully directed around the store instead of walking aimlessly around.

To use this analogy, you are designing a racetrack and not a runway. A racetrack design encourages customers to go around the store and be exposed to all the products in the store, whilst a runway encourages customer to move up and down the store in high speed.

Here now are some tips on designing your store to increase customer flow:

Positioning your checkout counters

The position of checkout counters is critical for controlling the movement of customers in your store. Generally customers walk away from checkout counters because checkout counters remind them that they are going to spend money.

Therefore, it is crucial that you position the checkout counter in such a way that it is not the first thing customers see when they enter the store. After they are relaxed, they will naturally gravitate towards it. The right positioning of your checkout counter can result in increased sales.

Control customer movement

You are designing to encourage customer movement around the store. To achieve this; products need to be strategically displayed to persuade shoppers to move from one end to the next and in the process view other products. The way to ensure this is to place essential products in different locations of the store.

Especially essential products such as:

- Milk
- Bread
- Sugar
- Toilet paper
- Detergent
- Coffee
- Beverages

Strategically locate these products around your store in order to force customers to walk around in search of them.

Make adequate use of sightlines

Sightlines are a very critical component for encouraging customer flow. They attract customer's attention as they move around the store and they generate curiosity. Strategically locating sightlines in your store would encourage customers to move around and get to know what products are on display.

Create destination departments

There needs to be destination departments in key locations of your store and ensure customers are aware of them. They need to be strategically located close to the entrance and exit points and in high traffic areas of the store.

Examples of such departments may be:

- The Power Tool Department
- The Seedling or Bedding Plants department
- The Ski Department

- The In-house Deli
- Lighting
- Shoe
- Electronics
- Technology

Use the right lighting system

At all times your customers need to be able to easily see as they walk around the store. Product areas need to be properly lit to attract their attention. When customers feel trapped or lost in your store they will leave immediately.

Create narrow aisles

Create narrow aisle space that would slow down customers as they walk around your store and get them to look at more products. However, the aisles have to be wide enough for the comfort of the customer. Wide aisle space encourages customers to move fast through them without actually browsing the products especially if they already know what they want to buy.

Strategically locate high demand products

High demand merchandise needs to be located at the end of the aisles. This encourages customers to walk pass other products before getting to them.

Display impulse items strategically

Display impulse buys, small and constantly in need and regularly purchased products close to checkout counter and in high traffic areas.

Strategically locate promotional products

Feature or promotional products should never be placed at the entrance to your store. When customers enter your store, they need time to adjust to the environment. They are less likely to pay careful attention to products that they see as they enter.

Do not neglect disabled customers

When designing your store, consideration has to be made for customers with disabilities and special needs. Aisles need to be wide enough to accommodate wheelchairs or mother with prams.

A successful retail store design strategy creates a store that leaves your customers with a happy experience. However it is essential that you regularly refresh your design to take into account and reflect changing trends.

Your store associates can play an important role in increasing customer flow and enhancing your customer experience. The quality of service and experience your customers receive will result in return customers.

Chapter Five

How To Choose Your Store Colour And Layout

Design is the most important aspect of a store layout. When the design is poor, the shopping experience of the customer can be ruined resulting in complaints and eventually loss of customers. The key to a workable design that attracts customers to your store is to determine the total customer experience you wish to achieve.

The appearance of a store is often fundamental to the success of that store. The most successful retailers maintain a consistent layout, colour scheme and other thematic elements that help customers recognise the organisation.

The colour and layout of a retail store can be the difference between a great shopping experience and one that results in a shopper exiting your store empty-handed.

In many stores, customers are unable to touch products that are in packaging. As a part of your store strategy, you need to think of ways of creating an interactive layout that provides customers an opportunity to have a feel of the products.

One way would be to display models of the products as was discussed in the case of Harrods' children section, to allow customers the opportunity of sampling products. An example will be to place batteries in electronic devices so that customers are able to sample them. This strategy alone can dramatically increase your sales.

A good store layout will not only help you influence customer's behaviour by properly designing customer flow, merchandise placement and the entire ambiance; it also provides you with an understanding of sale per square foot. This can help you properly determine the extent to which you are utilising your selling space.

Below is a breakdown of the benefits of having good store layout.

Layout your image

Your store is not only the theatre for the physical display of your products. It is also an outline of the image of your store. Like any business, image sells and your store image is more valuable than your merchandise. Having the right layout can enhance your overall image.

Predict customer buying behaviour

The strategic arrangement of fixtures, strategic placement of staircases, escalators and departments affect store traffic and the amount of time customers spend in your store. The longer customers stay in your store, the more likely is it that they will buy. Therefore, the goal of your store layout needs to be to keep customers as long as possible in your store.

A good example of strategically laying out a retail store to retain customers for longer in the store is the display strategy used by supermarkets and grocery retailers. They display essential products such as bread, milk and egg at the end of the store.

It forces customers to walk pass other products before reaching them. Department stores also use this strategy. By placing children department on the top floor of their store, they encourage customers to walk through other departments thus increasing the possibility of them buying other things as they walk.

Maximize selling space

You can measure the productivity of your sales space per square foot by monitoring the sales figure of each area in your store. Based on your assessment of the outcome of your measurement, if you notice that a specific area of the store is not meeting its sales goals, you can rearrange the fixtures and merchandises to improve the situation.

The objective of an effective store layout is to display as much merchandise as possible per square foot and ensure the merchandise is displayed to attract sales.

Ensure high value items are given priority when designing your store layout. Low ticket items can be displayed in such a way as to ensure they occupy minimum space.

Implement contextual display

The implementation of a contextual display is another way of making effective use of your display space. Products that are somewhat related to one another can be displayed in the same location. This is likely to trigger impulse buying and maximise the use of your selling space.

Also placing similar brands in the same section or displaying complementary products such as shirts and ties increases the possibility of sales and is a good use of display space.

Use layout to instigate positive emotions

Your store layout can determine the customer's emotion and sentiment they display while they are in your store. The emotions your store layout triggers in customers as they walk around would determine whether they buy or not.

If you intend to trigger a positive and relaxed feeling, your choice of colour, the arrangement of the merchandise and fixtures would determine whether you trigger your desired emotion in the customer.

Loss prevention

In the final analysis, your ultimate desire is to make a profit. The best way of making profit is to increase sales and reduce shrinkage. Creative arrangement of your merchandises, fixtures and layout can reduce the possibility of crime in your store.

The manner, in which your store is laid out, sends a signal to criminals, dishonest employees or shoplifters that you will not tolerate any form of criminal activity. It is very critical that you involve loss prevention in the preparation of your store design blueprint. By including loss prevention in the process you can benefit from expert advice on how to use your store layout to design out crime.

The importance of colour in store design

Colour is a very critical aspect of your store design. Colour is a very powerful intangible aspect of a design that if used properly can result in enormous benefit for the store.

On the other hand executed poorly, it can result in loss sales. Colour has a huge effect on the mood of people. Colour can stimulate happiness, relaxation, a feeling of comfort or it can result in anxiety and restlessness.

Consequently, as you make the decision on the colour of your store, the deciding factor has to be what emotion you want to trigger in your customers. Choosing a colour scheme to distinguish your store from the competition is somewhat of an art and a science, and it depends on your type of retail store and the image you wish to convey.

There are a lot of guidelines regarding colour application. For instance dark colour is inappropriate for small spaces or painting a space white makes it appear larger and grander.

Imagine how inviting your store would look with professionally painted signs, texture effects and the latest paint finishes. Or a super-modern digital print hangings, stencilled designs and murals that create a striking feature that will attract new customers to your store.

Colours such as blue, purple, white and green are believed to encourage a feeling of calm and relaxation. It is believed that stores decorated with these colours stimulate a feeling of rationalisation and positive thoughts in the minds of customers, resulting in them spending more in those stores.

Customers in stores with those colours are generally calmer, go about their shopping slowly and stay longer in the store.

On the other hand, stores with red or orange considered hot colours generate a feeling of anxiety and claustrophobia in their customers. Customers in those stores do not stay long because they feel uneasy, restless and impatient.

However, all colours have their pros and cons. Bright colours such as red and orange are excellent colours for attracting attention to your store. In most instances, the first thing a customer notices when on a shopping spree is not the name of the retailer or its brand logo but its colour.

How to determine a good colour and store layout?

Listed below are steps for determining your store's colour and layout:

Step One

It is very critical that every aspect of your store layout is taken into consideration during the planning stage of your store design. The essence of the layout is to reflect your store's image; therefore it has to be part and parcel of your store design blueprint.

Step Two

Decide on the type of atmosphere you want to have in your store. You might prefer your store to look feminine, sophisticated, masculine, child friendly, gothic or unisex.

Step Three

Choose the appropriate colour scheme for your target market. If your store is a lingerie store, you might want to go for a sultry, sensual feel. This would demand using colours such as black, cream, gold, deep pink and red, as opposed to blue, green or yellow.

When choosing walls and flooring colours, it is very important to keep the goal of the space usage in mind. If you intend on selling children products, warm and exhilarating colours would be appropriate.

Step Four

Offer multiple buying opportunities when customers are in your store. Create your design blueprint in a way that popular items are placed at the back of the store to ensure customers walk through the entire store. Display inexpensive and impulse items at the front of the store or close to the checkout counter.

Step Five

Make your store as easy as possible to navigate by placing clear signs in each section. Ensure products are accessible by using fixtures that are easy for customers to reach. When customers are unable to reach products, they might just leave without buying.

Step Four

Ensure you have adequate space for customers to walk freely across aisles. Narrow aisles create a feeling of entrapment. The front of the store should be more spacious than other areas because that is the where the highest level of traffic is located.

Step Five

Ensure high ticket items are displayed in secured cabinets to reduce the risk of theft. When customers want to see those items, a staff member should be available to open the cabinet for them.

Step Six

Select the appropriate lighting system. Store lighting systems would be dealt with in another chapter. However, it is important that you include the lighting system in your store design layout because light plays a crucial role in product presentation. A good lighting system can make a product appear more valuable than it actually is.

The layout and design you chose for your store needs to be based on the overall vision of your store. You first and foremost need to take into account your target market. It is the selection of your target market that would determine the type of layout and colour that would suit your store.

Chapter Six

The Best Retail Store Lighting System

Retailers tend to focus on ample lighting while paying scant attention to the quality of the light in their store. But the quality of light in your store is a very significant determinant of the success of your store. Good lighting is important for:

- Attracting customers into your store
- Guiding them through the store
- Helping them evaluate the products
- Helping your store associates complete sale swiftly and accurately

More than the above light is closely linked to:

- Increasing store sales
- Providing customers with a good impression of your type of store
- Increasing the perceived value of your products
- Creating a conducive shopping environment for your customers

The most common things taken into consideration whenever retailers think of ways of increasing sales are:

a) Increased advertising

b) Intensive promotion

c) New product line

d) Changing store fixtures

e) Relocating products

The lighting scheme of their store is never taken into consideration. A good quality lighting system in your store enhances the look of both the store and the display.

When your store appearance is enhanced because of good lighting customers are more likely to believe that the products in your store are of high quality. The core of marketing is perception…what the customer thinks about your store.

I am not suggesting you deceive your customers with lighting technology. What I am trying to point out is that good lighting increases the chances of customers wanting to enter your store.

Listed below are the most commonly used retail lighting systems:

Ambient Lighting

Figure 9: Ambient lighting aid shoppers movement around the store

Ambient lighting is the basic lighting system in a retail store that aids customers' movement around the store and helps them to evaluate products. Ambient lighting is just a basic lighting system; light that enables people to see clearly when they get on with mundane activity in a slightly dark area.

Accent Lighting

Figure 10: Accent Lighting is used to highlight a specific item in a displace

Accent lighting commonly known as "focus" lighting is used to draw attention to a few products in a retail store. This is particularly useful for highlighting high ticket or promotional products.

Accent lighting is the favoured lighting system of luxury retailers. That's because it allows them to highlight individual products in the store. Except for promotion accent lighting is not very useful in a low end store.

High Activity Lighting

Figure 11: High Activity Lighting focuses attention on a specific department

High Activity Lighting schemes are used to focus attention on a particular area of the store. Whilst accent light focuses on a specific product, High Activity Lights focus on specific areas. There might be areas of the store that are darker because of location or fixtures. High Activity Lights can be used to brighten up such areas.

High Activity Lights can also be used to promote a certain department or section of the store. If there is less traffic in certain areas of the store, High Activity Lights can be used to increase traffic to those areas by highlighting them.

Shelf and Case Lighting

Figure 12: Shelf and Case Lighting is used to illuminate display cabinet

Shelf and Case Lightings are used in display cabinets and shelves where certain high ticket or exclusive items are displayed. Shelf and Case Lighting serves two purposes: to ensure that the product is properly seen in the display case and to enhance the appearance of the product.

Perimeter and Valance Lighting

Figure 13: Perimeter and Valance Lighting is used for towers and tall shelves

The Perimeter lighting scheme is used for tall vertical shelving and displays. While a valance lighting scheme conceals the source of light on merchandise. Perimeter lights are often positioned in a way that they illuminate the vertical surfaces of the area.

Architectural Lighting

Figure 14: Architectural lighting highlights the design of a building

The Architectural lighting scheme is used to light up and highlight the architectural design of a building. Architectural lighting can be used on the inside or outside of a building. Luxury retailers use Architectural lighting to show up the shape of their retail design.

Task Lighting

Figure 15: Task Lighting is used to conduct specific task

Task lights are installed specifically for use by staff assigned to specific tasks. They can be installed at the checkout counter, customer services counter or in specific areas of the store where store associates are expected to perform specific tasks.

Your lighting scheme needs to help customers to see what you sell and your store associates perform their duties well.

Be aware that Illumination of your store is a major factor in your customer's buying decision. In most instances shoppers will not buy a product if they have not had the opportunity to properly evaluate it and establish its specific attributes such as colour, texture and quality.

Your store lighting must also be good enough for customers to be able to read the price tag and labels of products.

Generally, a good lighting level in a store is about 75 foot candle and a bit higher level if your target market is older people.

The decision as to which lighting system you choose for your store should be guided by the primary objectives of any retail lighting system:

Attracting customers into your store

The style of lighting you have in your store should signal to your customers that your store is open for business. Your lighting system needs to breed curiosity in shoppers as they pass by your store.

Guide them through the store

You lighting needs to guide customers around the store and to specific areas you would like them to see. When you make effective use of accent lighting, you can control customers' movement within the store and persuade them to go from one section to the next to see what's on display.

Helping the customers evaluate the products

An adequately lit area makes it easier for customers to weigh up products and make buying decisions. When customers have the opportunity to checkout products without any form of hindrance, they are more likely to make a buying decision.

Helping your store associates complete sale swiftly and accurately

The point-of-sale, customer service desk, changing rooms and all other points of the store where store associates are expected to serve customers, need to be well lit so they could perform their duties easily.

Below are some important factors to consider when installing lighting system in your store:

- Colour rendering index/colour temperature

- Contrast/accent/highlight
- Daylight Integration/regulator
- Direct glare/reflected glare
- Image/style
- Modelling of objects/shadows
- Visual priority/organization
- Quantity of light on vertical displays
- Quantity of light on horizontal surfaces
- Use high colour rendering lights

When selecting your lighting system, you need to ensure that the types of bulbs you choose are those that make product colours appear as natural as possible.

What to look for when selecting your light system?

The specification on the packaging that indicates it renders colours accurately.

Colour rendering index (CRI) is specified on bulb packaging or on manufacturer's catalogues.

CRI of lights ranges from one to as high as a hundred. For your store, you need to select lights with a CRI of 80 or above. Some standard halogen incandescent, fluorescent and metal halide lights meet the 80 and above CRI value.

Lighting fixtures should limit glare

Ensure that the type of lighting system you choose limit the customer's view of the light louvers, baffles, and lenses. When light shines in the eyes of the customer, it creates discomfort and reduces the customer's desire to stay in your store.

Lighting system such as accent Lighting should be aimed directly at the products. Spot lights with small beams should be selected as well as fixtures in which the light is dipped into the fixture's opening. Ensure that lights are not aimed directly toward the aisles or doorways to prevent it shining into the eyes on customers.

Properly distribute light

Light has to be evenly distributed throughout your store. The entrance, areas between aisles and display have to be well lit to ensure customers are able to see products properly as they move around the store.

Since most products are displayed vertically, it is essential that the lighting system you select can properly light vertical surfaces. This is possible by using adjustable fixtures that can be directed toward shelves and vertical displays or by selecting ceiling-mounted fixtures that are designed for all round coverage.

Attract customers to products with light

Figure 16: A good lighting system makes products appear more attractive and valuable

A good lighting system can be an effective way of attracting customer's attention to specific areas of your store you would like them to go.

It is a mistake to use spot or accent Light such as halogen reflector lamps all over your store. They make the store appear cluttered and can sometimes confuse the customers. Light should be effectively used to attract customers and adequate in specific areas such as checkout or customer service counters.

Below is a further guide for choosing and implementing an effective lighting system:

Place the lighting source as close as possible to the merchandise.

For ambient lighting, use efficient diffusers such as fluorescents.

For accent lighting, use narrow beam spotlights such as Halogen PARs or Low-Voltage MR-16s.

Brighten up your store aisles with spill light from the accented merchandising areas or displays.

Use the lightest colours on the interior surfaces of shelving.

Ensure you use organized patterns of lighting fixtures. Chaotic patterns may confuse, agitate or fatigue the customers.

Ensure you use high colour rendering lamps for both ambient and task lighting

In clothing stores the lights must be adequate in sales areas and dressing rooms so that customers can see how the items look prior to purchasing.

While lighting must attract customers to your store, the objective needs to be to enable customers to read signage and move unhindered throughout the store. The level and quality of the illumination in your store will create a lasting impression on your customers and will be the key to whether they will return to your store.

Be aware that the lighting system is as dynamic as the products you display; therefore you cannot be rigid about it. You need to understand that certain displays and seasons might require a different lighting system.

Consequently, it is extremely important that you ensure that your store designers make provisions for such events.

Chapter Seven

How To Wow Customers With Creative Storefront Design

As a part of my research for this book, I stopped in at shopping centres around the UK. That was in January, one of the most important months in the sales calendar for the retail industry. The January sales come in the wake of Christmas and more particularly the Boxing Day sales.

Retailers sell and conjure massive discounts as they bid to unload excess end of year stock before they restock and update lines for the New Year. So shoppers are wooed with discounts of up to 70%.

What happens during these sales is every business rule is broken. Instead of focusing on profit, retailers focus entirely on sales. I couldn't help but observe that there was total disregard for the security of the merchandises and storefronts ceased to function as instruments of marketing.

However, the first two points are not the topics of discussion in this chapter, therefore, I will limit my discussion to the third aspect which is the storefront.

A retail storefront serves three main purposes:

1) It is the image of the store and all that it represents
2) It serves as an effective marketing tool to attract customers into the store
3) It is the point of transition between the outside world and your store

Despite the significance of the storefront in retailing, too many retailers pay scant attention to this area. They spend most of their time getting the inside of their store design right and completely ignore the storefront.

For a start, the storefront window is the most expensive part of a retail space. It is considered to be equal to one third of the entire cost of the store rental. In his book: "Window and Interior Display – The Principles of Visual Merchandising", Robert Kretschmer reveals that *"A small store out of the high-rent district, with a rental of $100 a month, would put a yearly rental value of $400 on its window. Windows of the higher-class stores are often considered to be worth £20,000 a year or more. In New York City stores such as Macy's value their window space at more than $100,000 a year".*

Kretschmer feels that the value of the store window is based on the number of people who pass by it each day. "So" he explains *"in towns with populations ranging from 2500 to 25,000, window passers-by number between 372 per hour and 4,464 per day."*

To calculate the current value of your storefront, try *Kretschmer's* formula:

"The value of a window space is the basis upon which a charge against the merchandise department is determined. Two factors must be taken into consideration: (1) the comparative importance of the space and (2) the actual rental cost of the window. For example a store with 16 windows, 4 of them on a main thoroughfare and the remaining 12 on a side street carrying less traffic, would of course, place a higher rating on its 4 front windows.

Windows one through four, on the main thoroughfare, would be rated highest in importance and value. Then, starting with window

5 and down the side street to window 16; each window would diminish in value.

Assuming that each of the 4 front windows had an equal rental and budget cost of $18,200 a year, each department using one of them would be charged at that rate, or $60.66 a day (on the basis of 300 working days a year). Window number 16, with a rental and budget cost of only $4800 a year, would draw only $16.00 a day from the departments using it".

Based upon the above formula, calculate the value of your own storefront. You will grasp the importance of maximising its value.

In the beginning of the chapter, I outlined the result of my own research into storefront usage in the UK.

Figure 17: Even though the store front is the most valuable space in a retail store, most retailers do not make good use of the space

Figure 18: Successful retailers know the value of their storefront

When I took a trip around shopping centres in the UK, one observation I made which Kretschmer confirms in his book was that tier one retailers made proper use of their store windows. While tier two and independent retailers not knowing the value of their storefront, covered their entire storefront with discount signs.

> To quote Kretschmer again: *"the modern high-class store shows a few carefully chosen articles in a single unit of a display to create an atmosphere of quality and exclusivity of style. A store of this type may devote forty weeks a year to these simple, exclusive showings.*
>
> *Yet the same store can cram a window full of merchandise for its January white sale or its August housewares clearance or for its Christmas toy displays, without sacrificing any of its dignity.*
>
> *The character of the store is so firmly established by its regular display policy that these sporadic outbursts of high-powered sales promotions only accentuate the high-class rating of the store. The so called middle-class store has a tendency to crowd its display just a little.*
>
> *This store puts more merchandise in its windows than the high-class store, yet at the same time it strives to imitate the style of the quality store. Its aim then must be to attract some of the cream of the trade while still catering to the very profitable middle class."*

The lower-class store directs its attention mainly to the purchaser of low-priced goods. The windows of such a store are often crowded up to the hilt, more like the old-time general store. You can further identify this type of store by its inferior price tickets and gaudy show cards and banners.

Figures (1-5) show images of a tier one retailer. Figures (6-7) show images of tier two and three retailers during the January sales period. As you can see while tier one retailers only have a few sales signs in their windows, tier two and independent retailers cover their entire storefront with sale signs.

One of the most important elements of a storefront display is to tell the story of the display. Having a sign that says 70% as the only storefront display of a retail store tells customers that particular retailer has no story to tell.

The general consensus in marketing is that people buy emotionally but justify their decisions rationally. To appeal to their emotions, you should have more than your price displayed at your storefront. Price is a single factor for which people buy and in most cases it's the least of the reasons why people buy.

Thirty up to 40% of customers will buy on price alone. However, up to 70% will buy on the basis of convenience, good customer experience and quality. Therefore, in order to persuade the large majority of people to enter your store, you need more than 70% discount stickers displayed at your storefront.

First and foremost you need to have a storefront display that triggers all of their buying emotions.

How to design an attractive storefront

The storefront needs to convey a clear message about your brand and products. The message must be simple, unambiguous and to the point that shoppers get it as they walk by. The decision to take a closer look at your display or enter your store depends on how attractive he (she) finds your storefront display.

There is a direct correlation between your storefront design and customer traffic. Traffic will increase if your storefront is designed to catch the eyes and get in to the psyche of shoppers as they pass by your store.

The power of your storefront is as much in its signage, as it is in its lighting; interactive window displays and visual merchandise displays.

Storefronts vary from one store to another. Depending on the type of retailer it can include wholesale stores, kiosks, barrows, market stalls and internet based retail stores. However, all retail storefronts must meet the following three objectives:

    a) Attract shoppers attention

    b) Entice shoppers to enter the store

    c) Persuade them to buy

To meet the above objectives your storefront design must above all else, *represent your store image.*

Your storefronts should be an expression of your store's image. Your storefront has to be design in such a way that it expresses your store's individual identity.

Storefront entrance

Your door location and design are essential components of your storefront. They are the customer's transition from the outside world to your store. Your doors should place customers in the frame of mind of the type of experience they are about to receive. Consequently, it is advisable that doors provide direct link from the sidewalks or streets and should create a unique experience that distinguishes your store from other stores.

Storefront materials

Every component of your storefront needs to be purposefully designed to achieve your objective of attracting customer's attention. All materials used in the design need to be well thought through and of the highest quality. Your window needs to be designed in such a way that it creates a visual connection between the inside and outside of your store. Your entire storefront needs to be well glassed.

The most appropriate materials for a storefront are:

- Wood
- Metal
- Brick
- Stone
- Glass
- Concrete

Your storefront lighting system

A well-lit storefront is a must for the right store image. Effective lighting is good for merchandise displays as well as the safety of your customer and the general public. Sign lighting, including flat-mounted signs, blade and banner signs ought to be lit with covered or down lighting.

Lighting fixtures need to be positioned in such a way that they focus on the products on display not the window or street. When lighting fixtures are not positioned well, they either distract from the display or allow shadows that interfere with the display.

Your awnings

If your store has awnings ensure it is periodically cleaned to maintain the veracity of fabrics; seam and colour. Periodic cleaner also avoids the unnecessary expense of replacement. The awnings can be used as an effective marketing and image building tool. By placing information about your store on it you add feel to the streets cape and variety to the building façade.

It also saves the storefront displays from sun. Design and position should balance the scale of the store facade design.

The best types of awnings are retractable or open side as opposed to vinyl or internally lit awnings.

Signage

Your storefront signage illuminates the outside of your store and attracts customers like moths to a flame. Here the lighting also builds a sense of branding and brand engagement. The signage peeps into the souls of customers and creates a connection between them and your storefront signage.

This helps in the creation of brand awareness and brand loyalty. Your storefront signage needs to be incorporated into your entire storefront design and the store design itself.

Strategies for designing an attractive store

Display your finest products in your storefront window

Display your best and newest collection of products in your storefront window. However, avoid the temptation of cluttering the display with too many items. This would only confuse your customers. Displaying a few items with adequate space around them will allow each product to stand out. Ensure that the theme of the season is clearly visible in the display. Changing the theme of your displays on a constant basis will bring an aura of newness to the display.

Maintain a clean storefront

Your storefront ought to be clean and tidy at all times. You need to ensure that glass windows are sparkling clean to increase visibility; bricks and mortar buildings are pressure washed, wooden buildings are treated with vanish with a gloss finish and litter, leaves or any types of dirt is constantly removed from your store entrance.

Encourage curiosity with sidewalk sales

Extending your display to outside of your store, for example in the centre of the shopping centre, stirs curiosity. For loss prevention reasons, ensure the products displayed outside of your store are in inexpensive. Where ever possible display dummies. Remember the goal is to stimulate curiosity not to facilitate theft.

Make promotion and discount visible

This might seem to run contrary to what I said in an earlier chapter about displaying huge sales signs on your storefront. I am not suggesting that you display large signs that prevent shoppers from seeing your displays. There needs to be a balance between advertising and display. You need to ensure that customers are able to see the products on display while at the same time in a distinct yet visible manner make them aware of promotions and special offers.

Decorate storefront with plants

If possible enhance your storefront with plants. Placing plants at the entrance of your store sends very warm message of welcome to your customer and make them feel at home in your store.

There is almost a mystical or magical connection between humans and plants. Plants stimulate our natural senses especially in towns and cities, people want to have the opportunity to get closer to nature. Therefore, just having plants at the entrance of your store is enough to attract customers to your store.

Steps for designing an attractive store

Step One
Ensure your storefront is made entirely of glass with focal points, wooden cubes and shelves for merchandise.

Step Two
Fit awnings to protect shoppers viewing your displays, from rain, sun or snow.

Step Three
Install attractive and informative signage that is visible from the other side of the road and is easy to read. Signs should be hung on the outside of the building, front door and windows.

Step Four
Decorate the pavement of the door front with attractive tiles and ensure that door frames are big enough for all sizes of customers.

Step Five
Install an adequate lighting system at your storefront. Ensure proper lighting on display and the entrance as a whole.

Step Six
Paint your storefront with a vibrant colour; hang seasonal banners; flags or holiday decoration. Just do anything that would make your storefront standout.

Remember your storefront is the best and most inexpensive marketing tool at your disposal. Make full use of it and make sure that every decision you make about your storefront design is based on sound marketing principles.

Chapter Eight

How To Choose The Right Materials For Store Design

Design of a building starts with the concept or reason the building is to be designed. The next step is the development of the blueprint followed by the purchasing of the materials to construct the building.

Each of these aspects of a building is equally important because without the concept, the blueprint would not be created and without the materials the building would not be built.

In the last few chapters, we have dealt with the concept and the blueprint. This chapter is about showing you the best materials to use in the creation of a magnificent store design and why they are the best.

Retailing like any other business is very competitive. To compete in a crowded field, victory is possible once you have the ability to stand out from the crowd. Like most things in life, the difference between success and failure depends on doing the little things better than the rest of the field. In retailing one of those little things is to ensure that you acquire the right materials for your store design.

The three areas of your store design you really need to focus on are:

- Ceiling
- Walls
- Floor

In the rest of this chapter, I will introduce the most commonly used ceilings, walls and floors in retail store design and explain the benefits of using them.

Ceiling

I am quite aware that not a lot of people entering retail store raise their head to see how the ceiling looks. I promise you, there are a lot of people who will notice if your ceiling is not impressive. It is curious how thing like this works. When things are right, it is taken for granted. However, when things go wrong everyone notice them.

I introduce the concept because as I dive into the most commonly used types of ceilings, there is the tendency for many retailers especially tier two and three retailers to belief that people would not notice their ceiling.

> *When your ceiling looks good, hardly anyone will pay attention to it. That is a fact. However, if it is not presentable everyone will notice it, remember that.*

Ceilings are classified in accordance with their appearance or construction:

Cathedral ceiling

Cathedral ceiling is a tall ceiling area similar to that used in churches

Dropped ceiling

Dropped ceilings are specifically used for aesthetic or practical purposes either to achieve a certain ceiling height or to provide space for piping.

Listed below are suggestions on what to consider as a good ceiling design:

Flat white ceiling

Figure 19: Flat white ceiling give the illusion of height

A flat white ceiling is necessary in a retail store with low ceiling. It gives the perception of height in a store with low ceiling.

Tin ceiling

Figure 20: Tin ceiling gives the store an elegant appearance

Tin ceilings can give your store an elegance appearance and draw customers' attention as they shop. The name tin ceilings originated from the material used for the ceiling during the Victorian era.

They are now available in different metallic finishes. Aluminium is the most commonly used type because unlike some other metals, aluminium does not corrode and is very light, flexible and reasonably priced.

Wooded ceiling

Figure 21: Wooded ceiling adds warmth and charm to the store

Using wooden panelling would add warmth and charm to your store and provide a subtle finish. Matching a wooden surface with other wooden surfaces such as wooden curtain poles or ornaments can result in a cohesive and stylish finish.

Acoustic Ceiling

Figure 22: Acoustic Ceiling are sound-absorbing ceiling

Acoustic ceiling tiles are sound-absorbing ceiling tiles dropped into grid metal strips suspended from the actual original ceiling of the store. They were originally developed by interior designers as a way of lowering ceilings and reducing the level of noise in a room.

In addition to reducing noise, acoustic ceilings can also conceal unattractive fixtures, wires and pipes that may be running along the ceiling of older buildings.

The following are the pros and cons of using acoustic ceilings:

Pros:

- Acoustic ceiling reduces sound between floors of building and inside the store making it comfortable for customers to carry on their shopping.
- Acoustic ceiling tiles are simple to maintain or replace and can be painted.

Cons:

- Panels can be easily damaged by moisture causing the panel to drop from the ceiling unexpectedly in extreme cases.

- Moisture damage show and dries leaving an unpleasant stain on the ceiling.

Gypsum board ceilings

Figure 23 & 24: Gypsum board ceilings are commonly used products

Gypsum board is a common product currently used for walls and ceilings in homes and stores. It is easy to install however, the installation of suspension system requires a professional installer.

Gypsum can be found in sedimentary rocks all around the world. A layer of gypsum sandwiched between two sheets of thick paper is known as Dry wall.

The pros and cons of gypsum board ceilings:

Pros:

- Gypsum board ceilings are relatively simple to install and are reasonably priced
- Gypsum ceiling tile provides variety of designs, acoustical and aesthetic qualities.

Cons:

- Gypsum board ceilings do not absorb sound very well.
- Gypsum board ceilings can be easily damaged. It is recommended you use chemically treated gypsum wallboard that is moisture resistant in a store that has high moisturised contents.

Plastic Ceiling

Figure 25: Plastic Ceiling are alternative to wood and tile

Plastic ceiling tiles are an alternative to wood or plaster tiles that are commonly used by a majority of retailers. Plastic ceilings are reasonably priced, strong and long lasting. They are very light in comparison to wood making it easier to work with them. They do not appear as elegant or presentable as acoustic tiles or gypsum board ceilings.

Aluminium Ceiling

Figure 26: Aluminium Ceiling will not rut or crack

Aluminium ceilings are very durable ceiling that would not rust or crack because they are made from a non-porous material. They are easy to install because they consist of different panels. They can be installed like acoustic ceiling and fitted to the main ceiling.

Walls

The decision of wall covering in your store should be based upon: style, ambience, theme, image and the practicality of maintenance. If you choose to paint your store, it is advisable to use washable paints.

The most commonly used materials for walls in a retail store are gypsum board (dry wall). Their surface has slots which allow pipes, cables and conduits to run through them. Retail walls are either full height or partial height.

Plaster walls can also be used in place of gypsum board. They can be moulded into different shapes enabling them to form curve or soffit walls which cannot be done with gypsum board walls. Plaster walls are more durable than gypsum board walls and can be used in other areas of the shopping centre.

Wall Covering

The most commonly used wall covering in retail space is painting. In addition to heavy-textured paints, the three main types of wall finishing are gloss, semi-gloss and flat.

Flat paints are suitable for walls, while gloss and semi-gloss are suitable for doors, trims and high contact areas.

Wall paper is another type of covering used in some retail stores. Wall papers need to be located in less contact areas; probably close to the ceilings.

Wood

Figure 27: A combination of soft and hard wooden walls are commonly used

Oak, red or white wood are the most common types of wooden wall finishing in retail stores. Combinations of hard and soft woods are constantly used depending on the preference of the retailer. Hard wood include walnut, rosewood, mahogany, ash, oak and teak, while softwoods are pine, birch, cedar and redwood.

Hardboard, metal and plastic wall panelling

Figure 28: Hardboard panelling is an inexpensive thin particle board

Hardboard panelling is an inexpensive thin particle board about a quarter inch thick, composing materials that simulate solid wood. They can also be found in laminated tambour created to achieve batter effect.

Panelling or laminated plastic made from three quarter inch particle board layers of plastics which can be custom designed for individual retail stores. Plastic laminates are very durable and available in different colours, finishes and patterns and easy to clean but susceptible to chipping at the corners.

Metal laminates are also very durable especially when laminated to particle board. They are available in different types and finishes, stainless steel, aluminium, copper and brass.

Glass Walls

Figure 29: Glass is not easy to work with

Mirrors are used to create the illusion of extra space or reflect images. Mirrors are available in clear, grey and bronze finishes and are about a quarter thick. Glass is not particularly easy to work with, therefore the design needs to be uncomplicated.

Tile Walls

Figure 30: Tile Walls is durable and offers great degree of flexibility

Ceramic tiles can also be used as a wall finishing and are available in different sizes, shapes and colours. Terrazo is also very durable wall finishing that offers great degree of flexibility.

Flooring

Flooring is another very important component of retail store design. Unlike the ceiling, customers actually look at the flooring when they enter the store, therefore, it is imperative that you lay good flooring in your store.

Carpeting is the most widely used flooring type in the retail industry for the obvious reason that it is reasonably priced and comes in a variety of colours and textures and it has significant sound absorbing properties.

Other flooring materials used are:

- Resilient floors
- Wooded floors
- Non-resilient floors

Ceramic tile flooring

Figure 31: Ceramic tile is a very durable surface used for any type of application

Ceramic tile is a very durable surface that is recommended for basically any type of application. Ceramic is water resistant and there are porcelain tiles which are frost resistant and frost proof in some cases.

Ceramic tiles are so far the favourite retail flooring because they are highly resistant to moisture, stain and wear. They are generally produced in larger sizes and are suitable for large retail areas.

Vinyl composition flooring

Figure 32: Vinyl composition tiles are also widely used because they are very durable

Vinyl composition tiles are also widely used because they are very durable and the tiles bump flush together.

There are two types of vinyl floors:

Printed vinyl containing fillers of durability are made by imprinting a design on a film over a vinyl base.

Solid vinyl is widely preferred in high-traffic retail stores as the colour and pattern go through the entire thickness.

Eco tile flooring

Figure 33: Eco tile is an attractive and hardwearing interlocking floor tile

Eco tile is an attractive and hardwearing interlocking floor tile. It is designed to allow quick and simple glue less installation. They are thick and durable and are popular amongst retailers. Eco tile floor finishes are also low maintenance and last significantly longer than conventional vinyl or any other carpet alternative.

Listed below are tips for choosing your store materials:

- Select materials that are modern
- Select materials that are extremely durable
- Select materials that are quick and easy to install

- Select materials with good anti-slip properties
- Select materials that are easy to clean and maintain
- Select materials that are dynamic can be easily changed if the situation demands
- Select materials that are ideal for oily substrates

Chapter Nine

How To Design A Profitably Retail Store

In chapter two, I outlined the three factors responsible for Harrods phenomenal success as:

- Good store design
- Attractive visual merchandise display
- Effective loss prevention strategy

The subject of loss prevention is something that has never been taken seriously by the retail industry even though the industry spends billions each year on loss prevention. In fact in the last ten years, loss prevention spending has increased tremendously. In 2011 retail spending on loss prevention rose to $128 billion, however, in the same period retail shrinkage rose to $119 billion.

So why is it that despite the huge amount spent on loss prevention, retail shrinkage continues to rise?

To answer this question, let's take a peek into Harrods loss prevention strategy.

Harrods store design and visual merchandising displays are definitely factors in its success. However, the key factor responsible for Harrods' success is its ability to remain profitable. And in business, profit is king.

In retail the formula for making profit is to increase sales and reduce shrinkage.

Increasing sales requires good store design and attractive visual merchandising. Reducing shrinkage requires an effective loss prevention strategy.

So what do Harrods and most successful retailers have over the rest in the retail industry? It is their ability to simultaneously increase sales and reduce shrinkage. Most retailers know how to increase sales, but when it comes to reducing their shrinkage, they are challenged.

Getting these two right is the fundamental principle of retail success. No retailer can succeed without simultaneously increasing sales and reducing shrinkage.

Why does shrinkage reduction or loss prevention measures fail in most retail organisations?

Loss prevention measures fail as a result of the following:

- Lack of understanding of the subject
- Senior management's failure to prioritise
- Outsourcing loss prevention without a mechanism for accountability
- Inexperienced loss prevention managers
- Ineffective use of loss prevention technology

Harrods is the first retail store that I have ever entered that has no visible blind spots. I am not suggesting that there are absolutely no blind spots as I managed to spot a few.

However, the difference with other stores is that Harrods' blind spots are invisible to the untrained eyes.

Anyone deciding to shoplift in Harrods would have to be:

- A professional shoplifter or part of an organised retail crime syndicate
- Really brave
- Really stupid

Products are displayed in such a manner that each department seems wide open. Store employees standing at one end of a department have a clear view of the entire department.

There is CCTV in every corner of the store. In addition to electronic surveillance store assistants buzz around like bees and make it difficult for anyone who might be intending on shoplift.

I am not saying that it is impossible to shoplift from Harrods. Far from that, shoplifting prevention requires the implementation of a combination of strategies. However, by adopting their type of store design, displaying their products in the manner that they are displayed and taking other loss prevention measures, Harrods has drastically reduced the possibility of shoplifting.

Now contrast Harrods loss prevention strategy with a top ten UK retailer that I once worked for as a store detective.

A few years back, I was employed as a store detective for a leading retailer in the UK. On my very first day at work, whilst in the middle of briefing with the officer I was relieving, I noticed a couple walk into the store and head towards the coat section.

I stood there perplexed as I witnessed the lady remove one of the coats from the hanger, try it on, and then casually walk to the exit with her partner and scurry into the waiting getaway car. £900 walked out the door with such incredible ease, made me think "Holy cow! How can this sort of thing happen in broad daylight?"

The answer was actually quite apparent: The coats were prominently displayed right close to the exit.

Keeping this experience as a vivid reminder, any time I was assigned to a different store, I took great care to walk around and look for high ticket items that were not securely displayed. I would call the store manager over and advise that the items be relocated to more secure locations within the store. To my disbelief, most managers failed to take my advice – in their eyes, I am merely a store detective. What did I know about proper merchandising?

As a second example: I was working at a store in London Colney, immediately upon entering the store I noticed coats worth £250 prominently displayed near the store entrance. I located the store manager and expressed my concern to him.

I even joked with him how even the CIA Director at the time, George Tenant, could not possibly protect those coats where they were positioned. This manager ignored my warning. A few hours later, some of the coats were stolen, just as I had predicted.

When I approached the manager again, I figured he would pay more attention to me now that my gloomy prediction had come true. Once again, he failed to heed my warning only paying attention to me after 20 out of the 25 coats had been stolen.

At this same location, there are two big retailers who shared a single toilet facility located outside of both stores. Shoplifters knew this and would steal from one store, head to the direction of the toilet, pass through the other store and escape. When they were stopped and questioned by our store security, they would mention they were on their way to the toilet.

They were technically correct about the direction they were heading given the location of the toilet. The location of the toilet caused both stores to lose thousands pounds to shoplifting. Yet neither store's management could pin-point the location of the toilet as one of the primary causes of their shrinkage.

I share these stories with you to emphasize a very important point: Shoplifting occurs in most retail stores simply because it is allowed to take place.

> *Shoplifting is a crime of opportunity, eliminate the opportunity and you reduce its possibility.*

To increase sales yet fail to reduce profit draining activities is false economy. Many retailers feel loss prevention is something that they could do if they had the resources. The reality is: it is something that you cannot afford not to do because no retailer can become profitable without implementing effective loss prevention measures.

Inexperienced loss prevention managers

Ninety to 95% of retail loss prevention department managers are ex-service personnel. As a result of their law enforcement background, they take the law enforcement approach to their work. They focus mainly on arresting shoplifters and dishonest employees.

While it is true that shoplifting and employee theft accounts for almost 70% of retail shrinkage, they are not the sole cause of shrinkage. Furthermore, shoplifting and employee dishonesty cannot be tackled by solely arresting individuals. Preventative measures such as good store design and visual merchandise displays, as I mentioned in the case of Harrods, are the key to shrinkage reduction.

However, due to the fact that the majority of retail loss prevention managers know very little about store design and visual merchandising, they are unable to incorporate these aspects into their loss prevention strategies. As a result most loss prevention measures fail.

"The average retailer makes a 1% net profit out of each dollar and the average industry shrinkage percentage is 2.6%. This means that shrinkage is almost three times the average retailer's profit margin. By reducing retail shrinkage to 50% – from 2.6 cents to 1.3 cents, a retailer could more than double his profits: from 1 cent to 2.3 cents". (Crosset Company newsletter, June 2010)

Outsource Loss Prevention

Some retailers outsource their loss prevention department to outside contractors. As laudable as this may seem, it is a seriously flawed idea because retailers are sometimes incapable of clearly articulating their expected outcome.

When a job is outsourced, there is usually an expected outcome. However, if the retailer outsourcing the job cannot articulate their expected outcome, it is difficult to hold the contractor accountable.

Wal-Mart founder Sam Walton once described retail shrinkage as a "profit killer". He was right. High shrinkage is responsible for the death of many retail organisations.

The benefit of a good store design is to increase sales with the use of attractive merchandising display. However, attractive display does not necessarily mean designing your store without developing mechanism for crime prevention.

As you develop your store design blueprint, you need to ensure that the safety of the products is paramount. In the final analysis you are in business to make profit. You cannot make profit if you increase sales at the expense of the security of your products.

Without losing the original purpose of your store design, you can apply changes to the way fixtures are arranged in your store in order to decrease the chances of theft.

One way of doing this is to locate smaller items in places that are visible to employees. Furthermore, positioning employees in key areas of the store is a good shoplifting prevention strategy.

Larger products need to be placed in small quantities to prevent the store from appearing cluttered. Poor display of large products can obscure the view of employees and increase the possibility for shoplifting.

Aisles and shelves need to be properly labelled to ensure customers can easily and quickly locate products.

In addition to labelling, installing proper lighting will attract buyers to products as well as allow your employees to observe the surroundings more effectively.

There is no fail proof way of preventing shoplifting. However, the installation of security systems such as CCTV and mirrors can reduce incidence of shoplifting in your store. Security mirrors optimize employee's view of the store and reduce blind spots.

How to increase your sales and simultaneously increase your profit?

The following are effective steps for increasing sales and profit with a good store design:

Step 1:

Locate smaller products close to areas that employees frequently visit to reduce the risk of shoplifting.

Step 2:

Reduce the number of large products on display to allow store employees unhindered views of the store.

Step 3:

Position employees in key locations of the store to increase overall security.

Step 4:

Security mirrors in the store to reduce blind spots and increase surveillance.

Step 5:

Use CCTV in areas that are not regularly frequented by employees and place high ticket products under cameras.

Step 6:

Ensure your loss prevention department is involved in the planning of your store design blueprint.

Years ago, shoplifting was conducted by homeless and drug addicts wanting to feed their habit. Today shoplifting is conducted by retail crime gangs using more sophisticated methods, never before seen in the industry. Within four minutes, an organised retail crime gang could steal seven thousand pounds worth of products from your store.

Think about this when developing your store design blueprint.

Chapter Ten

The Best Store Design Technologies

Technology can enhance the process of your store design and enable you to achieve your objectives of increasing sales and profit. However, in order to derive the maximum benefit from any technology; it is essential that you choose the most appropriate technology for your store and target market.

There is no one size fit all when it comes to the acquisition and implementation of technology. Consequently, prior to the acquisition of store design technology, it is imperative that you give consideration to the desired outcome of the technology.

Here are seven questions you should answer prior to investing in store design technology:

1) What are the types of store design technologies available?
2) What are their functionalities including features and benefits?
3) What constraints do they diminish?
4) Where can they be sourced?
5) What policies and procedures helped you to operate without those technologies?
6) What policies and procedures should you put in place now to adapt to the new technologies?
7) Are the technologies future-proof?

Answering the above questions would guide you in your decision of selecting the most appreciated store design technologies for your store.

The use of technology is essential for any retail operation. Whatever the size of the retail store, technology has both tangible and intangible benefits and helps to increase profit, increase productivity and improve customer satisfaction.

In order to provide convenience and a unique shopping experience for your customers, listed below are examples of the latest retail technologies in the market:

Information kiosk:

- Provides information on locating products in a store
- Is valuable for displaying promotional and advertising information
- It can be used in a shopping centre to show location of stores

Satellite navigation software:

- Helps shoppers find products by using an app that runs on Smart phones
- Speeds up shopping by showing customers a 3-D store map and the shortest route to pick up everything they need

Sensormatic Safer Electronic Article Surveillance (EAS) Solutions:

- With Sensormatic Safer Electronic Article Surveillance customers now have the freedom to openly select high value items without waiting for store associates. Specific area of the store could be fitted with the system.
- High ticket items have safe lock to prevent shoplifting

Radio Frequency Identification (RFID technology):

- Provides retailers with an advanced bar coding system as no line-of-sight is required to read a product with an RFID tag

- Automates the retail supply chain, reducing labour costs, human error and time spent checking in products
- Is less susceptible to damage as it is placed on a product or embedded in plastic to withstand harsh environmental conditions such as moisture, exposure to chemicals and outdoors

Point-Of-Sale system (POS Technology)

- Records sales as they occur and provides detailed inventory report
- Solves a variety of operational and record-keeping problems
- Can be customised to meet your specific requirements
- Can quickly locate sale prices and costs of all products
- Help determine the causes of shrinkage
- Records marked downs and discounts
- Tracks promotion successfully and easily
- Accurately reveals the effect of promotions
- Helps monitor store associate activity and productivity
- Ensures product prices are consistent in multiple retail operations
- Can be integrated into other software providers packages such as expenses, payroll or staff attendance software
- Helps in effective workflow distribution to accurately monitor activity of each store associate
- Provides accurate customer profile: buying behaviour, addresses or emails
- Facilitates an easy payment method

A lot of new retail technologies are constantly introduced into the market. I have chosen to focus on the main ones that can be integrated into other types of technologies. Most importantly, they can all be used for loss prevention purposes. It is a fact of life that new technologies are obsolete within three years of invention.

This means that you need to always be on the look-out for new technologies that would increase your productive capacity, staff productivity and ultimately your profit margin.

Part Two
Visual Merchandising Display

Chapter One

The Psychology Of Visual Merchandising Display

Visual merchandising is basically a truncation for marketing in retail. Selling takes place when customers and shoppers show interest in a product and the intention to buy a product on display.

However, before arriving at that conclusion; the individual needs to be sold which is why merchandising is very critical for a retail store. Most people do not buy because they are uninterested in a product or service been sold to them. And it is very difficult to sell to an unmotivated person.

So how do you motivate a person?

You do that by selling them what they want.

This brings us to the next question.

What does everyone want?

In marketing we are taught to believe that everyone wants a different thing.

This statement is true to an extent but it's not quite true. Human psychology has not changed since the dawn of time. The same desires we harboured when we lived in caves, we still hold dear today.

Every shopper, client or customer wants basically the following three things:

> ➤ Result

> ➢ Solution

> ➢ Relief from something

These three things manifest themselves in the form of the products and services we choose to buy. However, in the final analysis when someone takes out his credit card to buy a product or service no matter what that product or service is, they are doing so to satisfy all or at least one of the above.

Being aware of that, as you prepare to display your merchandise, the questions that need to be going through your mind are the following:

- Which one of the above three are you marketing to satisfy in a particular display?
- When someone passes your shop window, and they take a glimpse of your display, what emotion are you aiming to trigger?
- What result should they imagine the display is going to produce for them?
- What solution should they think your display would provide?
- Finally what pain is the display going to relieve?

This is classic marketing 101.

Your merchandise does not necessarily have to produce those results for the shopper; it just needs to produce the perception of the result in the shoppers' mind.

But there is a catch: the person creating the display needs to know the benefit behind the benefit (the solution the shopper is seeking).

It is only when your visual merchandiser know the benefit behind the benefit will they be able to create a beautiful attractive display that captivates their targeted audience.

I will use La Senza as an example. A woman passing by a La Senza store, spots a sexy lingerie on display in the window; her first thought is: I will look sexy in that underwear or that bra looks to be just right for me.

Figure 1: Think of the benefit behind the benefit in your display

But here is the interesting part, she would like the bra to prop up her cleavage not because she just wants them cleavage propped up. She wants her cleavage propped up to attract the attention of the opposite sex. (I must add a disclaimer that here that I am not trying to be sexist; I am just using this as an example).

Therefore as a visual merchandiser your aim in creating a display for that lady should not be about the cleavage, but the opposite sex. Your goal needs to be to match the thinking process that lady in your display.

Do not create a display to appeal to the beauty of her breast but the impression that the beautiful breast will have – on the opposite sex!

You see that with travel agencies. When you enter a travel agency, what do you see?

The images of a beautiful beach, with a couple or an individual sun bathing and a stunning hotel in the background.

No mention of the eight hours flight to get there, not to mention the two hours check in time at the airport, screaming kids on the airplane, the rude cabin crew and lest I forget...the sleeping air controller.

There is never any mention of those. All they paint for you is the picture of perfect get away that you cannot wait to buy.

As a visual merchandiser, this is the type of picture you want to paint with your display. A major part of visual merchandising is being able to analyse people's thought process.

The human thought process is complex and irrational. Even though he tries to rationalise his actions with artificial explanations of his environment, the reality this: we all do things for the same three reasons:

➢ Status
➢ Survival
➢ Sex

I am aware this might sound like a little over simplistic explanation of the complexity of the human thought process. However, the more you understand your target market, the more you will come to the conclusion that indeed all human actions can be reduced to the three.

As a visual merchandiser your ability to capture these three in your presentation is the key to your success.

The human has three brains:

➢ Reptile
➢ Mammal

> ➤ Thinker

The problem we face as humans, those three brains are not integrated. They all work separately and the thinking part of the brain is the least dominant of three, which why our thinking process is in most cases, irrational.

In his ground breaking book: "Blink", author Malcolm Glawell brilliantly illustrates this point when he introduces the concept of "the power of thin slicing" and "rapid cognition" which is the type of thinking process that occurs in a blink of an eye.

Thin-slicing is a psychological term for the ability to find patterns in events based upon minimal information. It means making rapid decisions with the least amount of information.

When someone walks through a shopping mall of three hundred stores or on a busy High Street on Saturday afternoon, his mind races and he thinks at a fast rate.

The decision as to which store he enters is made in the blink of an eye. It depends on the merchandise display that catches his attention. Except of course if he had pre-planned a visit to a particular store; he is thin slicing each store as he walks along.

Many of our actions, behaviour and thinking originate from the adaptive unconscious which the majority of us are unaware of. Almost all the time, our decisions are based upon triggers from the unconscious.

The good news is that other humans are capable of altering these unconscious biases just by tinkering with miniature details.

Malcolm Glawell spoke about the tinkering or social engineering process in his first book "The Tipping Point". In "The Tipping Point" he outlines minute details of product packaging for example, that causes a product to tip (increase sales).

The retail landscape is changing rapidly. Endless choices, interruptions and information from all directions are either confusing customers or overwhelming them.

As the shopper walks through the shopping mall, there are a gazillion things going through his mind. Yours is not the only display in the shopping mall neither is it not the only display he has seen on that day.

There are clusters of information and displays all around them. Therefore your job as a visual merchandiser is to ensure that yours stand tall above the rest. That can only be done when you understand the psychology and design your display to suit customers' desire.

People don't like to be sold but they love to buy, therefore your visual presentation should sell to them without appearing to sell to them.

The most effective visual merchandise displays are those that speak directly to a customer's desire for:

> Result
> Solution
> Relief from something

Remember! It is all about:

Status

Survival

Sex

How to implement the psychology of a visual merchandise display

Starbucks has become the favourite hangout for many professionals. But if you went into a Starbucks you will notice that there is nothing special about it. It does not have special decoration or a seat that makes it stand out from all other cafés yet that's exactly what it does…standout above the rest of the cafés.

Apple retail stores are simple, there is nothing sophisticated and stylish about them yet they standout stores in any mall. Apple stores are fast becoming a favourite hangout for shoppers.

So what is it about Starbucks or Apple that makes them stand out?

Answer: Simplicity and elegance!

The fundamental principle that underpins an effective presentation is clarity of message and enhancement. Every presentation carries a message. It can be explicit or implicit; so long as it speaks to a targeted audience.

It is very important that your audience gets the message that your presentation is sending to them.

When the London 2012 logo was unveiled the head of the London 2012 organising committee went through pains of explaining what the logo depicted to the British public.

Figure 2: London 2012 Olympic logo confused everyone

Except for him and probably the designers of the logo, no one else in the UK seemed to have understood the logo. As far as most Brits were concerned, it might have been Greek or symbols from some Hindu alphabet.

When people were interviewed about what they made of the logo, some people described it as children drawing from a nursery...

For some it was an angry person expressing their feelings.

Not a single person associated it with the Olympics. That is a classic example of a presentation gone wrong.

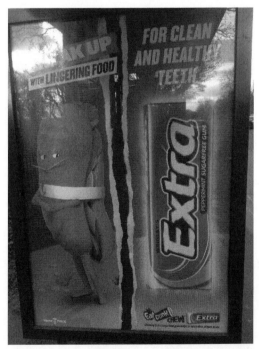

Figure 3: what is the connection between bread and chewing gum?

This is the image of an ad I noticed at the bus stop on my way to the post office. It is an ad for a chewing gum. But as you can see it has the image of a big loaf of bread and the chewing gum on the side.

What exactly is the relation between a chewing gum and a loaf of bread?

As I walked around I constantly see ads on billboards and street corners that do not speak to any specific target audience.

Walking around the shopping mall and in retail store I cannot help but notice several visual merchandise displays even in large retailers that speak to no one in particular.

When creating a visual merchandise display you need to adhere to the following guidelines:

- The display has to be unambiguous so that it can be instantly understood by the targeted audience
- The display must invoke confidence in the brand
- The most important element of the display has to be the biggest and dominant feature of the display

Every single component of the display must be a part of the message you are trying to convey. There can be no component of the display that is there simply to make the display beautiful and more attractive; it must be a part of the overall message.

Colours have to be used sparingly. Colours have to complement one another and be in sync with the rest of the products in the store.

Visual Merchandise Psychology Process

Step One

Know thy customers – Identify your target market.

Step Two

Find out what result, solution and relief they are aiming to achieve with your product.

Step Three

Find the benefit behind the benefit they are trying to achieve (the guy with the muscular body for which they need that bra to prop up their cleavage).

Step Four

Create a visual display that speaks directly to their needs.

How to identify your target market

This is marketing 101 which every business should already know, therefore I am not going dig deep into it.

However, small retailers who might not have the luxury of hiring an expert visual merchandiser might find the following steps helpful:

Step One

After creating the display, speak to staff members and ask them to describe the display for you in their own words. If they explain it in words that you expect your customers to use then you know you have nailed it. This needs to be done every single time you tinker with the display.

Step Two

Speak to your customers – ask them what they think about the display. Ask them what message the display sends to them. If your customers describe your display using words that indicate that they got it, you know you have achieved your objectives.

Step Three

Ask your customers why they buy certain things from your store. When you know why they buy, you will know the result they are trying to achieve with your products.

Step Four

To be able to ascertain the benefit behind the benefit, find out what they intend to do with your products after they have bought it.

For example if a lady came to your store to buy lingerie. By asking her a few probing but un-intrusive questions as she tries them on, you will know if she is single and going out on a date or she is dressing for her spouse.

The more similar answers you receive the easier it would be to present your display to suite them.

Finally ensure your display does not look like the London 2012 logo. It should not confuse your audience; it needs to speak directly to their needs. When they look at it...blink they need to see the result, solution and relief they seek.

Chapter Two

How To Use Visual Merchandising To Increase Sales

Retail success depends on the image you create in your customer's mind about your merchandise as well as your provision of good customer services. Good visual merchandising also helps to create a positive customer image about your store and your products.

All of that results in increases sales.

But retailers tend to overlook the role visual merchandising plays in increasing sales.

Within the last few decades, the retail industry has recognised the role of visual merchandising display in increasing sales.

This is especially true for supermarkets that have mastered the art of visual merchandising display to the point of excellence.

Visual Merchandising display in a retail store:

- Enables consumers to easily locate products
- Keeps customers updated on the latest trends
- Influences customer buying decision
- Creates a pleasant shopping experience

Visual Merchandising display is basically what the shoppers sees either when passing by a retail store or when they are inside the store. It creates a positive image of the store which results in attention, interest, desire and action on the part of the customer.

Simply defined visual merchandising display is the art and science of displaying products to influence shoppers buying decision.

The most aggressive application of visual merchandise displays is used by larger retailers. For instance, sport brands such as Reebok spend 25% of their advertising on point of sale merchandising.

Furthermore, there has been a significant increase in impulse buying of certain products: that is directly attributed ingenuous visual merchandising display.

How to use visual merchandise to increase sales

Known in retail as the "silent salesperson", a good visual merchandising display:

- Presents the product to shoppers
- Invites the shoppers to get closer to the product
- Encourages shoppers to make a purchase
- Tells shoppers everything they need to know about products without the need to make inquiries

Visual Merchandising is a proven formula for increasing retail sales and customer satisfaction. It makes it easier for customers to see products on display as they walk around the store and aids in locating products easily.

The following are the three display structure used in retail stores. A retailer may choose to use the three structures in depending on his product range or he could use any of the three depending on his target market:

- Store-Front
- Window Display
- Found-Space Display

The most important element of visual merchandising display is the shop window display. The shop window display attracts shoppers as they walk pass and entice them to enter the store. There are lots of people who might have no intention of shopping on a particular day. However, the attractiveness of your window display could entice them into your store.

Display windows are usually facing the shopping mall or main shopping street and are geared towards attracting passers-by and enticing them to enter a retail store.

The storefront display is designed to build your brand image and tell the right story of your organisation. When developing the concept for your storefront, create the design from the customer's prospective.

Figure 4: The storefront display is designed to build your brand image and tell the right story of your organisation

You basically need to enter the customer's mind and ask yourself the question:

> What would my customers see when they look at my storefront display?
>
> What would they feel as they pass by my storefront?

The answers to those questions should inform your display design and structure.

When planning a window display take into consideration the following:

- The building façade
- The street
- Your target market and their perceptions
- Color harmony
- Lighting
- Viewing angles

Window displays are more successful when a central theme is carried throughout the display; whether the featured products are fashion-oriented, institutional or promotional in nature.

Window displays need to be constantly updated, preferably on a weekly basis or as often as possible. This sends a message to customers that there is always something new going on in the store.

Showcase Display

Figure 5: Showcase Displays feature expensive merchandises

Showcase Displays feature expensive merchandises retailers do not want to be seen in the front store window. They are usually exclusive items that require high security measures. These displays are usually located in high traffic areas in the store to ensure maximum customer attention. The lesser the items in the display, the more the perceived value, resulting in higher priced.

Found-Space Display

Figure 6: Found-Space Displays are displays of products at less prominent areas of the store

Found-Space Displays are displays of products at less prominent areas of the store, such as the top of shelves. When done right, they support your brand image and reiterate the story you want to tell with the display.

Below are points to consider when creating store displays for increased sales:

Install signage

Figure 7: Store signage needs to be appropriately installed

Store signage needs to be appropriately installed and placed in a position that allows shoppers to read the information written on them from across the aisle. A sign is a silent salesperson and a huge part of the shopper's first impression of your store.

Like Apple simplicity, clarity, elegance and legibility need to be the rule of thumb.

Use the appropriate colour

Figure 8: Your colour usage will significantly contribute to shopper's impression of your store

Your colour usage will significantly contribute to shopper's impression of your store as they pass by it. The store colour needs to be suitably chosen as it can influence your customer's mood.

The wall colours need to correspond with the carpet, floor tiles or the fixtures.

Lighting system

Figure 9: Lighting increases the visibility of the merchandise

The store should be appropriately lit and well ventilated. Lighting increases the visibility of the merchandise. A properly lit store contributes to the promotion of specific products and the store's image.

Store window lights should be strong enough to overcome the reflections from outside.

Contextual Product Display

Figure 10: Group together products in their respective racks

Group together products in their respective racks and place associated labels on the same shelves. This helps your customers locate products easily. The merchandise should be appropriately and neatly placed and should not fall off the shelves.

The latest trend items should be cleverly displayed on the shelves to attract customers and entice them to buy. Expensive and unique products should be placed on the right side of the store as most people are right handed and tend to gravitate towards the right side of the store.

Old merchandise should be removed as quickly as practically possible and placed on sale to create an atmosphere of constant freshness in the store.

Identify the right furniture and fixtures

Figure 11: All unnecessary furniture should be removed

All unnecessary furniture should be removed to create enough space for customers to move freely in the store. The more comfortable your store, the higher your chances of retaining customers, which will result in increased sales.

Maintaining an area for spouses or children to read or play and for physically challenged kids or elderly customers to rest also contributes to a good customer experience.

Providing resting space is a difficult concept to sell to store planners because of the cost of retail space. However, the payoff far outweighs the cost as the longer shoppers stay in your store, the higher the chances of them buying.

A changing room is an important component of a clothing store as it increases the possibility of the customer buying if they have had the chance of trying the cloth and it fits them well.

Separate changing rooms for male and female or a comfortable non-gender specific open space with individual cubicles will suffice.

Maintain good ambiance

Figure 12: The store ambience is essential for attracting new customers and retaining existing ones

Playing music that appeals to your target market can have a positive effect on your customers. Loud music is not advisable as it hinders effective communication between the customer and store associates.

Playing music that appeals to your target market is another strategy for keeping customers longer in your store.

The store ambience is also essential for attracting new customers and retaining existing ones. Customers shy away from untidy stores; therefore, ensure your store is tidy at all times.

The friendlier and more relaxing you can make your store, the longer your customers will stay and eventually make purchase.

Sometimes the store's appearance is more important than products in terms of a customer's decision to enter your store. Ensure your store entrance is welcoming; that your visual merchandise display tells the story of your store and merchandise display is resulting in higher sales.

How to implement a good visual merchandise display that increases sales

The following are the basic steps for creating visual merchandise display that increases sales:

Step One
Select a theme that tells the story

There needs to always be a theme or story that is being communicated to your potential customers in your display. Develop a theme around the reason why you decide to display some specific product in the window.

Who are the characters in your display?

Where are they going and why?

How old are they?

What jobs do they do?

What merchandise would help you tell your product story better?

If the story is about living a healthy lifestyle, what could you integrate into your theme to help you silently make this point in the display?

If your story is about Christmas, Valentine or outdoor adventure, what are the details that will make your story come alive?

You can take your story to a whole new level with the use of props and mannequins. Just as if you were writing a story, your display needs to answer these questions:

How old are your target market?

What do they do?

Where are they going?

What season is it?

You can also provide each mannequin a name to bring them to life. The key is to clearly understand who you are creating the display for and what message you want to convey to them through the display.

Step Two
Know thy customer

One of the major reasons for the failure of most retail ventures is that most retailers do not know their target market. This is marketing 101: It is critical for your success as a business. If you do not know who you serve, you might not be serving anyone.

> Who are your costumers?
>
> Are they teenagers, young professionals, college students or young couples?
>
> Are they housewives?
>
> Are they Single mums?
>
> Are they women in their 40's with lots of discretionary income?
>
> Do your customers want a bargain or are they looking for something unique?
>
> What interests them?

Answering the above questions will ensure that the message of your display is clearly understood by your target market. If your display does not target a particular segment of your market, it will not sell.

Step Three
Identify your Competitors

It is critical that you know who your competitors are; their product offering and service provision. By having an understanding of the strength and weaknesses of your competition, you can better prepare a display that either directly rivals or is better than theirs.

Competitive analysis is the key to the success of any business. Knowing the strength and weaknesses of your competition is a key element in your success as a retailer.

Step Four
Choose the right products for your store window

Your storefront is a window to your store. The products displayed their, provide potential customers an idea of the products inside the store. Consequently, it is imperative that you choose the products that are displayed in the shop window carefully.

You need to display products that are the most representative of products in your store.

Ensure that products that are displayed in the storefront are available in the store. It does not speak well of your store if shoppers are attracted to the store because of products they see in the storefront display but when they enter the store to buy that product, it is unavailable. Remember that the unavailability of product can result in a frustrated and unhappy customer.

Do not overcrowd the storefront with too much merchandise. The message you are trying to send to potential customers could be lost in an overcrowded window. Window displays should be in complete harmony with the entire atmosphere of the store.

Step Five
Observe the effect of display on your customers

An effective way to attract customers is to have good exterior and interior displays. As customers pass by your display, you need to have a procedure for measuring the effect of your display on them.

Does your display window inspire your customers?

Is it pleasing to the eye and does it have a welcoming effect?

Ensure you display your merchandise as it would be used in a real life scenario and that it is kept simple but striking to have a great impact.

Ensure that your window display can be seen from a distance to draw your potential customers inside your store. You might have the most creative idea, however, if you are incapable of displaying it in such a way that it grabs your shoppers attention as they pass by your store, you have defeated the purpose of the display.

The key to increasing retail sales; is an impressive and eye catching presentation of merchandise that attracts shoppers as they pass by your store. Encouraging sales through creative visual merchandise displays is the key to keeping a customer interested in your store.

Chapter Three

Challenges Facing Visual Merchandisers

Visual Merchandising display is the science of displaying merchandise in a retail store and storefront in a bid to increase footfall in a retail store. Besides your store design, visual merchandise display is the best and most effective form of promoting your store.

The most important element of visual merchandising display is that it is on the spot adverting. If a shopper sees a product on display that they like; they can make a purchase immediately and you can make a sale on the spot.

The most important aspect of your visual merchandising display process is in the message. It has to be clear and consistent. When the message is clear, it eliminates the possibility of appealing to the wrong target market and providing a bad customer experience.

Getting your display right is critical for the success of your business. Your display must reflect the quality and price of the products on sale. If you sell high a quality product, but your store design and merchandise display do not match the high end clientele you are intent on attracting, you will lose your target market.

By the same token, if your store appears high end but you sell low qualify products; you will scare off your target market. Consequently, it is essential that you ensure that your display speaks clearly and unambiguously to your target market.

Creativity and the love of design are the two essential requirements for becoming a good visual merchandiser. As a visual merchandiser you need to have the ability to come up with creative ideas about how you would like your display to look.

You need to be a good story teller with a kid like imagination. You need to stay current about developments in your sector and stay in touch with other visual merchandisers to stay abreast of the latest trends.

Challenges visual merchandisers face

Visual merchandisers face a number of challenges that limit their ability to create displays that woo shoppers in to a store. A good visual merchandising display strategy can result in increased sales, increased staff productivity and reduced shrinkage which eventually lead to increased profit.

However, getting visual merchandising right can be a mammoth task for most retail organisations.

The dynamic of the target market is one of the greatest challenges facing visual merchandisers. The volatility of consumer behaviour creates a nightmarish scenario for visual merchandisers who have to constantly invent creative ways to attract potential customers' attention.

The constant development of new products, scarcity of display space allocation and the constant change in consumer preferences all add to the challenging environment for visual merchandisers.

Below is an outline of a few of the challenges that visual merchandisers face:

Too much new merchandise

Figure 13: New products are produced every single day

New products are produced every day. This is a nightmare for visual merchandisers who are responsible for finding display space on the shop floor for new merchandise. The merchandising of fabric is not as difficult as groceries.

Because clothing is seasonal. At the end of each season, clothes belonging to the past season are either sold off or taken to the warehouse. However, the same cannot be said of groceries.

Tones of new products are produced every single day and the supermarket tests most products to see if they will resonate with consumers. It is the work of the visual merchandiser to ensure that each new product is given a space in the store and are visible enough for customers to notice.

This can be a nightmarish scenario especially if it is a low value or bulky product. Placing low value products in high traffic areas is a waste of space. In the same token placing new products in locations where they are not very visible reduces the chances of them being sold. Striking a balance between visibility and space allocation is a huge challenge for visual merchandisers.

Solution

One way of dealing with this challenge is to:

Reserve a specific section of the store for testing products. The only products that will be displayed in this section would be new products. This would make it easy for both visual merchandisers and customers.

If customers are aware that a particular section of the store is specifically reserved for new products, adventure seeking customers would go straight there to look for new products. It also makes it easy for the retailers to quickly gauge customer reaction to the product.

If a product placed there is sold out quickly, the retailer just as quickly recognise the need to order additional supplies fast; and can now move the display to a permanent location in the store. When a new product is placed amongst other products, it can sometimes be difficult to get an accurate picture of its popularity; due to its lack of exposure.

If it is a clothing store, again a specific section of the store can be exclusively set aside for new fashion. Imagine the response that you would receive from customers. They will visit the store specifically to look for the latest fashion.

The creation of such section for new fashion trends will now be multi-purpose: it would serve as a testing lab for new trends; it would provide convenience for customers because they will be able to find things easily and it would serve as a magnet for attracting customers who are bent on keeping up with latest trends.

Limited Display Space

Figure 14: Retail space is expensive; therefore, every inch of the store's display space needs to be maximised

Retail space is expensive; therefore, every inch of the store's display space has to be used to its maximum. However, with the constant introduction of new products, even hyper stores struggle for space to accommodate all the new products.

To cluster products in a bid to create more space is never a good idea as the store would appear untidy. Even in a store where clothes are replaced seasonally, there are still lots of new fashions that constantly come on the market. Therefore, it really is a struggle for visual merchandisers to decide which clothing or product to give priority in the display.

Solution

The best solution would be to place as much variety as possible but in small quantities. Staff need to keep a constant watch on shelves to ensure that they are not empty or well faced up. If it is a clothing store, the same rule applies. As staff walk around the store, they need to keep their eyes open for empty hangers and spaces between clothes. Every space needs to be immediately refilled.

If it is in a grocery, products also need to be displayed in small quantities. However, the aim has to be to display as much products as possible. Staff need to ensure that no shelf is left empty. The retailer needs to assign a specific supervisor whose job it would be to walk the store every hour checking all shelves and fill gaps as they notice them.

Supplier demand Premium Spacing

Figure 15: Suppliers compete for prominent and high traffic display space

Suppliers compete to have their products displayed in the most prominent and high traffic locations in the store. Here you must be on alert for signs of a conflict of interest between senior management; visual merchandisers and other staff.

The decision as to where products are displayed is often determined by senior management and the supplier; not by the visual merchandiser. Sometimes, what the senior management view as appropriate could prove difficult for visual merchandisers to implement. These conflicting interests result in lack of coordination and cooperation.

In retail, suppliers pay for their products to be displayed in store. There are locations in each store that are considered premium areas: they are mostly high traffic areas. Every supplier wants their products to be displayed in those areas because of a higher probability of increased sales.

And suppliers are will to pay handsomely for the privilege. The problem is sometimes their products contrast with the rest of the products in the department and fitting in their products might reduce the space availability for other products.

Solution

Suppliers and retail senior management need to be educated on the function of visual merchandising display in a retail store. This would help them to make an informed decision about the location of products in the store. Visual merchandising display is showbiz.

The objective is to:

- Attract shoppers as they pass by the store
- Entice them to enter the store
- Retain them for longer in the store
- Persuade them to buy

In order to achieve the above objectives, the placement of products on the shop floor has to be purposefully done, not done haphazardly to favour a few products.

Product security

Figure 16: Product security is very essential

Retail crime; including shoplifting, is responsible for the demise of most retail ventures. Years ago, shoplifting was done by the homeless and drug addicts who wanted to feed their habits.

Currently, shoplifting is conducted by organised retail crime gangs using sophisticated methods never before seen in the retail industry. Retail is a business and business is about making profit. In order to make a profit, a retailer has to increase sales and reduce shrinkage.

One of the best ways of reducing shrinkage is through creative merchandising that does not facilitate the easy pilfering of products from the store. It is therefore essential that visual merchandisers know their role in loss prevention and shrinkage management. The objective of visual merchandising is to attract customers. However, there has to be a balance between attracting customers and protecting products on the shop floor. It is therefore vital for visual merchandisers to be trained in and kept up-to-date with the basics for linking visual merchandising with loss prevention.

If products are displayed with loss prevention in mind, it becomes more difficult for them to be easily removed from the store. However, if the loss prevention aspect of the process is not taken into consideration, the products are at risk when they are placed on the shop floor.

The changing retail environment

Figure 17: The changing retail environment

The internet has removed the monopolization of the factors of distribution once held by a few. In the new retail environment, an individual can run a multi-million pound retail operation from the back of his car as long as he has an internet connection.

It also means that a small factory owner operating from his spare bedroom in China can now compete with a multi-national retail organisation in the West. As it stands, the retail environment demands a different approach to visual merchandising display.

You can no longer continue to view visual merchandising display as just another component of your operation. Visual merchandising along with store design needs to be considered a key component of a retail operation.

Visual merchandising is free advertising for your store. However, despite the fact that it is free; in order for it to be effective, all the fundamentals of advertising need to apply.

In his book "Breakthrough Advertising" Eugene Schwartz wrote "This is the core of advertising—its fundamental function: To take an unformulated desire, and translate it into one vivid scene of fulfilment after another; to add the appeal of concrete satisfaction after satisfaction to the basic drive of that desire. To make sure that your prospect realizes everything that he is getting—everything that he is now leaving behind him—everything that he may possibly be missing"

Below is a list of the fundamental principles of advertising:

- "The only purpose of advertising is to make sales. It is profitable or unprofitable according to its actual sales. It is not for general effect. It is not to keep your name before the people. It is not primarily to aid your other salesmen. Treat it as a salesman. Force it to justify itself. Compare it with other salesmen. Figure its cost and result. Accept no excuses which good salesmen do not make. Then you will not go far wrong".

- "Human nature is perpetual. In most respects it is the same to-day as in the time of Caesar. So the principles of psychology are fixed and enduring. You will never need to unlearn what you learn about them".

- "Use pictures only to attract those who may profit you. Use them only when they form a better selling argument than the same amount of space set in type".

- "Changing people's habits is very expensive. A project which involves that must be seriously considered. To sell shaving soap to the peasants of Russia one would first need to change their beard wearing habits. The cost would be excessive".

- "Prevention is not a popular subject, however much it should be. People will do much to cure trouble, but people in general will do little to prevent it".

- "We must learn what a user spends a year, else we shall not know if users are worth the cost of getting".

- "We must learn the percentage of readers to whom our product appeals. We must often gather this data on classes. The percentages may differ on farms and in cities".

- "Competition must be considered. What are the forces against you? What have they in price or quality as well as claims to weigh against your appeal? What must you do, to win trade against them? What must you do to hold trade against them when you get it? How strongly are your rivals entrenched"?

- "Almost any question can be answered, cheaply, quickly and finally, by a test campaign. And that's the way to answer them — not by arguments around a table. Go to the court of last resort — the buyers of your product".

- "Consumers all over the world still buy products which promise them value for money, beauty, nutrition, real relief from suffering and social status".

How to Resolve Visual Merchandisers Challenges

The following steps can help to bring relief to visual merchandisers:

1. Make effective use of a planogram to address the challenges of constant new product flow into the market.
2. Study your target market very well to determine product preference.
3. Group products according to make, model and size to enable easy display.

4. Ensure high ticket products are given priority in the display process.

5. Create an illusion of display with a few products that appear to be a lot.

6. Display smaller numbers of each product, especially slow moving products and ensure you make maximum use of the display space allocated.

Chapter Four

How To Burst The Price Myth With Creative Merchandise Display

I visited Harrods for research for this book and my book on store design. Harrods, for anyone reading this book who might not know, is the Mecca for retailing. Royalty, A-list celebrities and the 'who's who' from around the world fly into London just to shop at Harrods.

You can now imagine my anticipation when I visited Harrods. In my mind everything in Harrods was made of gold. I was disappointed; when I noticed a toy bus I had purchased for my son from Asda, was also being sold in Harrods. It was exactly the same toy bus, in exactly the same packaging as the toy in Asda.

A question popped into my mind: why is it that exactly the same bus, probably manufactured in exactly the same factory in China, is sold in Harrods for twice the price that it is sold for in Asda?

The answer is decisively simple – Asda sells a 'toy bus, but Harrods sells a 'classy toy bus'.

There is a difference.

This is marketing 101: people buy emotionally but justify their decision logically.

Customers who shop at Harrods do not shop there to buy Harrods' products; they shop at Harrods to buy 'elegance and class.' Harrods sells them class.

Figure 18: Harrods customers buy 'elegance and class'

How do Harrods pull this off?

They achieve it with the combination of an elegant store design and attractive visual merchandising displays. When you move from one department to the next in Harrods, it is like moving from one store to another.

Their ability to use their store design to create the illusion of variation is one of the keys to Harrods' success. Harrods understand their customers; they know what their customers want so they design their store and display their products to satisfy the desires of their customers.

The common myth in the retail industry is that people buy more when merchandises are cheap. That is just a myth. In this new retail environment where the monopoly of the factors of distribution has been broken, no retail store can be cheaper than the internet. Even pound stores are not cheaper than the internet.

The main reason people still visit retail stores is either for convenience or to actually feel the products before purchasing them. Some people might visit a retail store just for the fun of shopping.

It is true that 30-40% of people will buy on the basis of price only. However, the large majority of people still buy on the basis of value and convenience.

I am a one click buyer in Amazon. I buy a lot of books because of my line of work. I was pleasantly surprised to learn that I could even buy white board and all my stationary from Amazon.

I cannot remember the last time that I entered a bookstore. I have a lot of friends like me who do the majority of their shopping on the internet. They shop for clothes and even groceries on the net.

Why would I and many of the people do our shopping over the internet?

We are sold on the convenience.

These days there are people who will check things up on the internet, but before placing an order on line; they visit a retail store to see how they look.

The 18th century was about speed of production in order to increase capacity. The 19th century focused on quality. With the increased in production leading to over capacity, the focus shifted from speed to quality.

In the 21st century the focus has shifted from quality to value and total customer experience. But many retailers have failed to grasp the concept.

Here is the secret, despite the fact that people conduct research on the internet, the large majority still don't trust information found on the internet.

That is why books are still highly rated even though the information in most books can be found on the internet.

People still trust other people and prefer to interact with people. So despite the internet, bricks and mortar retailing will still survive. However, there is a new dynamic and retailers need to understand this.

The consumer of today is better informed than the consumer of ten or twenty years ago. Consequently, today's retail staff need to be better informed than retail staff of ten or twenty years ago.

One cannot navigate the 21st century with a 19th century skill set – it will not work.

Richer Sounds a UK based electronic and entertainment retailer has been featured in the Guinness Book of Records for the past 20 years as having the highest sales per square foot of any retailer in the world.

Coincidentally, their staff continue to top the 'Which" survey for excellent customer service and product knowledge. They are not necessarily the cheapest entertainment retailer in the world but they are the most profitable. Why? Because of the total customer experience that customers receive when they visit their stores.

Since the economic crisis, many middle or low tier retail stores have gone bust or struggling to survive. Yet the luxury sector of the retail market remains buoyant.

Even in recession hit Greece and Spain, the luxury retail market continues to flourish. The explanation that most people would have for this is that the rich are getting richer.

Even though this might be true, this is not the main reason for the continuous buoyancy of the luxury retail market.

The explanation lies in the fact that luxury retailers take the concept of total customer experience to the extreme.

When you visit Harrods, there is staff within an arm's length of each and every customer. On the other hand when you visit some retail stores, you can hardly find anyone to speak to when you need help.

I know of retailers in the UK who advertise on billboards in prime locations around the country. However, when shoppers visit their stores, they can hardly find a staff member to serve them and those in the store might have absolutely no knowledge about the products in the store.

To succeed in the 21st century retail environment, it is the little things that make the difference. As a retailer if you still believe that price is what is going to entice people to your store and make you successful, you are on the wrong end of the stick. 21st century retail is about value and total customer experience.

So as a retailer your focus needs to be on value drive strategies. An essential component of a value driven strategy is an attractive visual merchandising display. As Michael Porter puts it, "cutting prices is usually insane if the competition can go as low as you can".

Maintaining pricing integrity can be challenging in the face of fierce competition. But it can turn out to be a smart business decision in the long run. The concept of value is perceptive.

What might constitute value to one person might not be that valuable to another. However, there is a universal perception about value that exists in the mind of every customer: *cheap is poor quality and expensive is high quality.*

Despite the fact that this concept has proven time and time again to be untrue, like most things in life, it is the perception that matters.

Below is a list of the pricing strategies currently been used by retailers?

Price-matching guarantee

Price-matching guarantee is mostly used by consumer and industrial retailers. Retailers using price-matching guarantee frequently state that they are the 'lowest' priced store, and they will match the competitors.

A store with price matching guarantee will not lose customers to price cuts from other retailers even if it charges higher price to its loyal customers. Price-matching guarantee is an anti-competitive tactic that warns competitors not to attempt to steal market share by undercutting price.

Price slashing

Price cutting is a price strategy used by retailers such as Wal-Mart under their so-called "rolling back prices" price technique to eliminate competition. The core of the strategy is to reduce prices to a level low enough to eliminate competition.

Retailers use this strategy to under-cut the competition and offer the best price to the consumer. The objective is not to sell at a loss, but to reduce price to a point that competition is unable to compete.

Discounting

Discounting is a pricing strategy favoured by most retailers. It is done in the form of coupons, advanced purchases, loyalty cards or bulk buying. Coupons and promotions give buyers an incentive to buy from certain retail stores.

For some customers taking advantage of discount offers can be an attractive proposition. However, for the retailer concerned, discounting of products is never a smart business strategy as it eats into their profit margin.

The following are steps that prevent the need for product discounting:

Step One

Identify and understand your target market.

Like in the case of Harrods, customers visit a particular store for a reason. Your job is to find out who your customers are and what they want.

Step Two

Instead of discounting your current line, you could consider resizing.

As an alternative to discounting their menu, Quiznos took to a decision to resize its sandwiches.

Thus it offered a lower price for the smaller size. Probably there are ways that you could repackage your products in ways that it makes financial sense to discount without eating into your profit margin.

Step Three

Emphasize benefits of the products instead of the price. There is no getting away from the fact that it is very difficult to differentiate one commodity from the other. But it can be done if the retailer places emphasis on other intangible aspects of the buying decision.

Step Four

Emphasize the soft aspect of your offering such as great customer service, knowledgeable staff, easy access to merchandise, easy to locate merchandise or an easy to navigate store.

This might sound trivial, but in marketing, it is the things that are overlooked that count. The everyday thing that you think might not be important to the customer may well be what is really important to them.

The price discounting game is a losing one, do not play it, it is not a good business strategy.

When developing your pricing strategy you need to analyse the market place for sensory acuity. It can be done through the following means:

Competitive analysis

Conduct a competitive analysis of the pricing structure of your competition. When analysing your competitor's prices, your focus should not only be on the amount they charge but also their offering. You need to examine their entire service provision to be able to make an accurate assessment of the reason behind their pricing structure.

Maintain the ceiling price

If you decide to go for the highest price point, ensure it is the ceiling price. The ceiling price is the maximum price the market can bear. It is the price point that if you went above, you might scare away your customers.

Be aware that the price that might be the highest price currently in the market may not be the ceiling price.

Adhere to price elasticity

Price elasticity gives the percentage change in quantity demanded in response to a one percent change in price.

Price elasticity is almost always negative. Only goods which do not conform to the law of demand have a positive PED.

In most cases, the demand for goods is said to be inelastic when the PED is less than one. What this means is that changes in price have a relatively small effect on the quantity of the goods demanded.

The demand for goods is said to be elastic when the PED is greater than one. This means that changes in price have a relatively large effect on the quantity of goods demanded. As you develop your pricing structure, pay attention to these fundamental principles.

The following are steps for implementing an effective pricing strategy; when setting your prices to avoid selling at a loss:

Step One
Determine you cost
Calculate the cost of the product and add corresponding overheads such as: rent, utility bills, staff salary and benefits, marketing, credit cards or bank fees and professional fees.

Step Two
Know competitors prices
After calculating your cost, you then need to check out your competitor's prices for similar products. It comes down once again to ceiling price. If you notice that your price is lower than that of your competition, you will want to check out their offering before drawing conclusions.

On the other hand, if your price is higher, you cannot just reduce your price to match your competitors and operate at a loss. You also need to check out their offering and supply chain.

It is possible that despite the fact that their price is lower than yours, your offering might be more valuable than theirs. If that is the case, you need to ensure that your marketing stresses the fact that your offering is better.

You also need to pay close attention to their supply chain. The reason most grocery retailers struggle to compete with the likes of Wal-Mart and Tesco is because they have stronger bargaining powers when negotiating with suppliers.

This makes it possible for them to drive down their prices. So maybe instead of attempting to go head to head with to bigger players in your market who have strong bargaining powers, you can try changing your offering.

Step Three
Know thy customers

If you understand your customers better than your competitors, you will know the types of price they can bear. Again it is not about the cost of the product; it is about the total customer experience when they enter your store.

Harrods sell the same made in China products, however, it is able to sell it twice the prices of other retailers in the UK because its customers do not only buy at Harrods because of the products, but also because of Harrods total customer experience.

Step Four
Take the market into consideration

It is the market that sets the final price. Your final price would be determined by what the market can bear. The best strategy for testing the market is to start at the highest possible price point.

If you notice that sales are not being made as a result of your price point, you reduce the price and test again. Continue the process until you arrive at a pricing equilibrium.

As you test your prices, ensure that you have an accurate system in place for measuring the result of your pricing test.

How to handle price wars

Price wars are common place in retail. As stated previously, price is the most common strategy for differentiation in retail. Prior to deciding on your course of action during or even before engaging in price wars, you first need to consider this question:

Is the current price of the competition a short-term promotional strategy or a long-term pricing strategy?

If after analyzing your competitor's pricing strategy you reach the conclusion that it is just a short-term promotional strategy instead of log-term pricing strategy, you can either choose to ignore it or develop your own short-term strategy to counter theirs.

On many occasions, a price war is declared because retailers fail to analyse their competitors pricing strategy well.

Below is a list of possible responses to a price war:

Reduce price

You can choose to reduce your own prices in response to the competition's pricing strategy. This would seem on the surface the most logical action to take, but doing so would result in reduction of your profit margin.

Maintain price

You could ignore your competitor and maintain your current pricing strategy and hope that your competitor has made a mistake. This is a risky strategy because if in the process your competitor manages to lure your customers into their store, there is no telling that they would return to your store when the price war is over.

Use split market pricing strategy

This strategy is basically using different price point for similar products. This can be done by restructuring your product offer to promote a certain aspect of the product as basic and another part as premium.

Change your offering

The most effective way of winning a price war is to change your offer and service provision. Providing additional services such as home delivery or free shipment can increase the value of your offering tremendously.

How to implement a value driven strategy?

The best antidote in a price driven market such as retail is to focus on a value driven strategy instead of a price driven strategy. As I pointed out in the case of Harrods and the luxury retail market that is flourishing despite the economic downturn, price is never a good differentiator; therefore it is imprudent for it to be used as a long-term business strategy.

In this 21st century customer centrist environment where the definition of value has shifted from seller to the customer; where competition is fierce and the monopolisation of the factors of distribution has been broken, leaving the field wide open for anyone to enter; success as a retailer would no longer be dependent on 19th century marketing strategies.

Succeeding in the 21st century retail requires rethinking your approach to services provision.

It is now about providing sustainable, durable, reliable and high quality products at reasonable price.

Thousands of retailers are going bust while a few are succeeding beyond their wildest imagination. The retailers that are succeeding understand that the 21st century customer is better informed than customers of the last few decades.

They understand that succeeding in the 21st century retail environment requires a different approach. As a retailer, if your desire is to succeed in the 21st century retail environment, your best course of action should be to update your current operational processes to reflect the realities of the new retail environment.

Below is a list of quality improvement processes used by the most successful companies in the world. Adapting these into your current modus operandi would bring your retail organisation in touch with the realities of the new retail environment.

Hoshin Kanri

Hoshin Kanri or policy deployment; is Japanese for strategically capturing and strengthening strategic goals and developing the means to bring the goals into reality.

Hoshin translated from Japanese to English means shining metal compass, or pointing the direction and Kanri means management or control. As the name suggests using Hoshin planning aligns an organisation toward focusing on the accomplishment of a single goal.

It is a strategic planning and strategic management methodology based on the concept that each person is an expert in his or her own job.

Japanese TQC (Total Quality Control) is designed to use the collective thinking power of all employees to make their organization the best in its field.

This concept was made popular in Japan by Professor Kaoru Ishikawa. In his book "What is Total Quality Control" he asserts that senior and middle managers need to be bold enough to delegate as much authority as possible.

Professor Ishikawa's also believes that a sure way to establish respect for humanity is to adopt management system in which all employees top to bottom participate in the decision making process.

Hoshin Kanri's real aim is to help companies:

- Create common goals
- Communicate those goals to every employee
- Involve all employees in the planning and execution of the plan for achieving the goals
- Create a mechanism for accountability for every participant

Kaizen

Kaizen is Japanese for continuous improvement or change for the better. It is a philosophy that focuses on continuously improving any process.

It can be applied to any work process whether it is manufacturing, engineering, sport, government, healthcare, banking and any on-going activity.

The main objective of kaizen is to eliminate waste and create a benchmark for constantly moving up from one stage to the next.

Kaizen is originally a Buddhist term which comes from the words "renew the heart and make it good".

The adoption of the Kaizen concept in any business demands a change in the very 'heart' of a corporate culture and structure. Kaizen requires businesses to intertwine their vision with every aspect their operational practices.

Kaizen gradual step-by-step process of improving every aspect of a business while at the same time developing employee skills through training and increased participation in the process.

The key areas Kaizen can be implemented in a retail environment are:

> Shop floor – GENBA,

> Product – GENBUTSU

> Training – GENJITSU

By pursuing improvements in the three 'GENs', a retailer is able to spot issues as they arise and can gradually make changes to the key operations – product, service and total customer experience.

Poka-Yoke

Poka-yoke is Japanese for mistake prevention or "mistake-proofing". A poka-yoke is any mechanism that helps a worker avoids mistakes.

The main objective of poka-yoke is to eliminate mistakes by taking preventative and corrective actions prior to an error occurring. Poka-yoke was adopted as a modus operandi by Shigeo Shingo of Toyota as a part of the Toyota Production System.

The fundamental of poka-yoke is to design behavior-shaping constraints into the working process, to prevent incorrect activities by employees.

Below is a list of ways of triggering the thinking process for improving your retail organization:

> The needs of the customer

> It is possible to improve anything

> Quality is the responsibility of all employees

> The employee assigned to a particular job knows more about the job than management

> People should be respected

> Teamwork is critical for success

> Differences should be respected

> Participation in results and commitment

> Support results in success
> Every employee makes the difference

This book is about visual merchandising so why have I taken the trouble of including information on price and quality improvement. As I have reiterated continuously, the 21st century retail environment is a new environment.

The old modus operandi of previous centuries will not work in the 21st century retail environment. To succeed in retail in this century demands a change from the old way of working.

Visual merchandising has always been perceived in terms of the design and presentation of products. The 21st century visual merchandiser needs to understand the reason behind the process and 21st century senior retail management needs to understand the bigger picture of visual merchandising.

It is no longer just about the presentation of products. It is the thinking process behind the presentation of products that matters the most.

Chapter Five

The Best Merchandise Display Strategy

Shelves and display spaces are the most valuable spaces in a retail store. Consequently, retailers tend to work hard to ensure they maximise return on investment on each square foot of store space.

They display as many products as possible to ensure the maximum utilisation of their display space. Displaying too many products can result in wastage, while displaying too few could result in loss of sales.

The trick is to strike the balance between the two: ensuring customers are able to easily find the products they went into the store to buy and in the process reducing shrinkage.

Visual merchandising display is basically the physical presentation of products for the purpose of increasing sales. Visual merchandising is essential for maintaining the balance between shelf and warehouse stock.

Visual merchandising display is commonly referred to as the silent salesman because a good display effectively sells the products.

The core objectives of visual merchandising are to:

- Enable shoppers to closely examine products
- Maintain the customer's interest in the product
- Encourage them to lower their psychological defences
- Make the purchasing decision easy

However, the most successful retailers do not view visual merchandising as just the display of products on the shop floor. They see it as a marketing tool.

Because they view visual merchandising as a marketing tool, when creating a display, they do not only focus on the physical aspect of placing the products on the shop floor or storefront, they focus on all aspect of the process.

In fact their main focus is on the thinking behind the process rather than the actual process of displaying the products. I will diverge here a little to make this point clearer.

I do a lot of internet marketing, for that I attend lots of internet marketing events taught by the most successful internet marketers in the world. In event after event that I have attended or bought, I continued to observe an interesting trend; the most successful internet marketers do not teach people how to succeed on the internet. Instead they teach marketing fundamentals.

The way they see it, like visual merchandising, the internet is only a vehicle through which they can apply timeless marketing fundamentals. The likes of Google, Facebook, YouTube, Amazon, eBay and many of the successful internet success stories are not successful because their ability to use the internet better than their competitors. They are successful because they applied timeless marketing principles using the internet as an instrument.

There is similar situation with social media. The myth goes that social media can generate loads of customers. As the most successful internet marketers know, social media does not bring anyone business or customers.

It only effective use is to draw traffic to a business's website, the business has to apply timeless marketing principles if it intend on converting those visitors into customers.

The principles of marketing like any principle have never changed. The application might change but the principle itself endures for ever. The fundamentals of marketing have never changed since the beginning of time because human behaviour has never changed since the beginning of time.

This is what one of the world's legendary marketing gurus Eugene Schwartz had to say about this point.

> *"Human nature is perpetual. In most respects it is the same today as in the time of Caesar. So the principles of psychology are fixed and enduring. You will never need to unlearn what you learn about them...Consumers all over the world still buy products which promise them value for money, beauty, nutrition, real relief from suffering and social status".*

Marketing is what determines the success and failure of any business. Your ability to acquire and retain customers at the most cost-effective rate would determine your level of success in your retail business.

In Value Migration, Adrian Slywotzky stated that:

> *"A business (model) design is the totality of how a company selects its customers, defines and differentiates its offerings (or responses), defines the tasks it will perform itself and those it will outsource, configures its resources, goes to market, creates utility for customers and captures profits. It is the entire system for delivering utility to customers and earning a profit from that activity".*

In their paper "while the term 'business model' is often used these days, it is seldom defined explicitly." Chesbrough and Rosenbloom point out that there are six specific functions of a business model:

- *Articulate the value proposition – the value created to users by using the product.*
- *Identify the market segment – to whom and for what purpose is the product useful; specify how revenue is generated by the firm.*
- *Define the value chain – the sequence of activities and information required to allow a company to design, produce, market, deliver and support its product or service.*
- *Estimate the cost structure and profit potential – using the value chain and value proposition identified.*
- *Describe the position of the firm with the value network – link suppliers, customers, counterparts and competitors.*
- *Formulate the competitive strategy – how will you gain and hold your competitive advantage over competitors or potential new entrants.*

Joan Magretta wrote in the Harvard Business Review in May 2002:

"A good business model answers Peter Drucker's age-old questions. Who is the customer? And what does the customer value? It also answers the fundamental questions every manager must ask. How do we make money in this business? What is the underlying economic logic that explains how we can deliver value to customers at an appropriate cost"?

As you make plans for your visual merchandise display I want you to give some thought to the above messages. The main objective of a visual merchandise display is to motivate customer interest in your products. Displays should also be able to provide information about the products; show customers how to use the product.

A good visual merchandise display strategy answers the following questions:

> Does the display fit your brand image?
> Is it attractive enough to capture the customers' attention?
> Does it have a story to tell to the customer?
> Does it have a clear and specific message for the customer?
> Is it focused on the product?
> Is the information of the display easy to read?
> Does the lighting system bring out the best in the display?
> Is the display well organised?

The answers to the above questions will result in:

> Increase footfall
> Increased impulse buying
> Good brand positioning
> Effective use of display space allocation

In the fiercely competitive retail market you need to ensure you provide your customers the total shopping experience they crave. Taking the time to think through your merchandise display process – applying fundamental marketing principles will provide you huge competitive advantage over your competitors.

What is a good merchandise display strategy?

So how can you influence your customer or potential customers' buying decision through the creative use of a visual merchandise display? You can do that by simply asking yourself:

What catches your attention and persuades you to enter a particular store amongst three hundred stores in a shopping centre?

An answer to this question would bring you closer to answering the question of how to influence your customer's buying decision.

A creative visual merchandise display must have the following:

Balance

Balance refers to the manner in which the products are arranged around an imaginary centerline. When the phrase formal balance is discussed in relation to a visual merchandise display, this means that a product is on one side of the line, and a similar product is displayed at the same distance from the line between both products in the display. Balance encompasses the symmetry and weight of products on two sides of a display.

Emphasis

Emphasis is using one product in the display as the centre of attraction. The product would be core of the display around which the rest of the display is arranged.

The emphasis in a display is where the potential customer is expected to look first and it is deliberately arranged by the visual merchandiser to be the most prominent component of the display. All good visual merchandise displays have an emphasis.

Proportion

Proportion is the dimension and spacing of products in a display. Proportion can refer to the relationship between the product used as emphasis and the rest of the products in the display.

When the word proportion is used in relation to a merchandise display, it refers to the relative association of every piece of the display in relation to the: distance, size, amount and degree of differentiation.

Rhythm

Rhythm is the measurement of systematised movement from one product to the next in a merchandise display. Rhythm is an inexplicit guide tactically placed in the display to guide the customer's eyes from product to product in the display back to front and/or side to side.

The rhythm is also necessary for leading the eyes of the customer from the product of emphasis to the rest of the products on display as they look at them.

Harmony

Harmony conveys the mood and emotions of the display. It is obviously the most important aspect of the display. However, because it is not a tangible object, its essence could be lost in the display. Harmony is the story and message within the products on display. It is what brings the display to life and gives it character.

There are self-service and full-service displays

Self-Service

The Self-service display is a display in which the products on display are the ones on sale. If customers see a product in the display that they like, they can select the product and take it to the checkout counter.

Full-Service

A full-service display on the other hand is a mock display of the products. The main products are kept in the warehouse or behind the customer services counter. If customers see a product in the display that they like, they need to call one of the store associates who will go and collect the product for them.

This sort of display is usually used for expensive or large products and it is frequently used in luxury and upscale retail environments.

Big retailers often use a combination of both self-service and full-service.

How to conduct a good merchandise display strategy

The two types of displays are window and interior displays.

Window Display

Window displays are merchandises displayed in the shop window to attract shoppers as they pass by the store. The main objectives of a window display is to attract shoppers attention and entice them to enter the store.

Consequently, window displays are often brightly and impressively colored and lit. Window displays are usually season and occasion related; for example a window display for Valentines would be done in red and white colours and hearts reflecting love.

Interior Display

An interior display as the name suggests is the display of merchandise inside the store. Interior displays are also strategically located in various locations of the store to attract customers' attention as they move from one part of the store to the next.

The main objectives of interior display are to increase customer desire for the merchandise, show what merchandises are available, and stimulate both impulse and planned buying.

There are three types of interior displays: Open; closed, and Point-of-Purchase.

Open Display

An open display is one in which customers have access to the merchandise. They can touch, feel and try on merchandises in an open display.

Closed Display

Closed displays are displays that restrict customer access. Merchandises are usually kept enclosed in display cabinets and behind the cashier checkout counters.

Point of Purchase Display

Point of Purchase Display refers to products that are displayed close to the checkout counter. The main objective of this display is to encourage impulse buying. The Point of Purchase Display can be used to introduce new products, announce special offers or stimulate "no brainer" purchases such as lip balms, pens and small items.

When planning your visual merchandise display, take the following into consideration:

Your Brand Image

Is the display consistent with your brand image?

As a retailer, you represent a certain image to the public.

That image needs to be reflected in all of your marketing materials, messages and visual merchandise displays.

As you plan your display, the question that needs to be core to the process is, does the design represent the brand image you are known for?

Your target market

The next point that needs to be considered is: does the design appeal to your target market? I am making the assumption that you already know your target market. So as you prepare your design story board, the question that your need to be asking is, does this message speak to our target market?

If the answer is yes, then your display is effective. If no, you will need to tweak it until it speaks directly to your target market.

What's the concept?

What is the concept of the display?

What would it be communicating to your target market?

The most effective displays are the ones in which the products are displayed exactly how they are to be used. It could be a clothing display in which the item is dressed on a mannequin the way some-one is expected to wear it or in a furniture store where furniture are arranged in a way that they are expected to be arranged in a room.

The display structure

Considerations have to be given to the area in which the display is to be located. The location of the display has a significant impact on how it is to be designed? In retail store displays are usually located in: windows, walls, cases, gondolas or islands. The specific area in which the display is to be located within the store would determine its size and shape.

Promotional displays

Displays created for promotional purposes need to be different from the rest of the displays in the store. Promotional displays need to be located in the front of the store for a short period after which they should be moved to the back of the store if you intend on carrying on the display for a long time.

Customers who are interested in bargains will find it no matter the area of the store it is located.

Your customers need to be treated to new and exciting displays every week to create a sense of freshness in their heads. Always ensure that you have enough products in stock during promotional periods to cater to customer demand.

The following steps for creating displays that would increase your sales:

Step One
Determine the goal of the display

Every display needs to have a specific goal. The questions with which to determine this are: Is the goal of the display to promote new products; to carry on promotion; to attract a new target market to your store?

There needs to be a goal for each and every display.

Step Two
Choose the right merchandise

The merchandise on display needs to reflect the types of merchandise you sell. To ensure this takes place, the questions you need to answer are:

Does the merchandise on display match the quality of your product?

Does it reflect your brand image?

Your merchandise displays need to contain the right product for the right time. If the display is for Valentine, every product on the display needs to be related to valentine.

Step Three
Choose a theme

Every display needs to have a theme. The theme of the display is the story behind the display. You need to be able to identify the message you want the display to send to your target market. The theme of your merchandising can be a way to communicate a seasonal message to your target market.

Step Four
Select props

Props are the items used in a merchandise display to physically support merchandises that form part of the display theme. Props are essential for strengthening the message of a display.

Prop characters are essential for determining the overall appearance and feel of a display hence the reason why it is essential to get the appropriate props for your display.

Step Five
Create a contextual display

Create contextual displays by merging similar products together. This makes buying decisions easier for customers. For example: putting together shirt and ties or shoes and socks.

When products are grouped together, they make it easier for customers to make their choice. It also results in increased sales as it encourages a lot impulse buying.

Step Six
Develop signs

Ensure your signage is visible enough to complement the merchandise on display. There needs to a balance on the amount of signage placed on a display to avoid confusion.

The objective of signage in a display is to provide information such as the price of the products on display. It needs to be brief and easy to read. Signage should also prompt customers to move around the store. The sign should basically covertly inform that there are more great products to be seen in the store.

Step Seven
Design the lighting

Your lighting system is the most important element of your display. You need to ensure that the lighting system used for your display is the most appropriate one. The lighting system is also very crucial for your display because the right lighting system enhances the appearance of the products.

A good lighting system can also create an illusion and make products in the display appear more valuable than they actually are.

The light should be enough to enable the customer to examine the display and read the signs related to it. You can use a spotlight to highlight specific items in the display.

Ensure the lighting system does not cause glare and shadows around the display area. This is done effectively when you have different lighting sources.

Finally, displays must be neat and simple.

A cluttered display sends a bad impression of your store.

A confusing display would result in poor sales.

Therefore, it is very important that displays are:

> Neat
>
> Uncluttered
>
> The display area clean

There are no unrelated things lying about

The objective of the display should be to:

Attract customers as they pass by the store

Entice them to enter the store

Retain them for longer in the store

Persuade them to buy

Remember visual merchandising display is first and foremost a marketing tool, therefore the design has to be infused with timeless fundamental marketing principles.

Chapter Six

How To Maximise Display Space Allocation With Creative Display

Maximising display space to achieve the maximum return on investment per square foot ought to be a main objective of your visual merchandising display strategy. The cost of retail space by square foot is on the increase. So too is the variation of products. Creative use of display space is particularly relevant for retailers who sell low value products.

There are only so many products that can be crammed on a shelf in a small retail space. This means that space needs to be used creatively, to result in maximum profit for the retailer.

What Is Creative Space Use?

Creative visual merchandise space is the efficient use of retail space to maximise its potential capacity while retaining the sense of present-ability. This allows the products for presentation to appear neat and eye catching to the passing customer.

The efficient use of retail display space has several benefits:

• The ability to stock more products
The more space you have to display merchandise the more products you can display in your store.

• More supplier support
With fierce competition in the retail marketplace, all suppliers want their products to be allocated a space in a store, preferably in the high

traffic areas. Consequently, suppliers are willing to bargain for marketing support and higher space rental just to get the space that they want.

• More organised and controlled displays

An organised and well-controlled display area results in the maximisation of space. When your store is well-organised it is easier to monitor your products. There is also less incidents of pilferage and theft.

• Increased consumer satisfaction

Aside from good quality products and services that the store offers, availability is also very important to the consumer. Product prices prove irrelevant in comparison to convenience and quality.

• Increased sales and profit

Increased customer satisfaction results in increased sales and profit. Word of mouth advertisement based on personal experience is the oldest but still the most effective marketing tool.

For example, grocery items displayed on end caps and promotional merchandise situated near the store entrance are more likely to attract customers' attention than if they are positioned in a side aisle or in the back of the store.

• It helps prevent out-of stock and inadvertently lose sales

When you display your merchandise properly on the shop floor, they can be easily monitored by staff to ensure that the spaces are constantly refilled. In most cases when customers notice that a product is not on a display only a few customers who desperately need the item would bother to ask store associates. The majority would just assume that it is unavailable in the store and go somewhere else and buy.

The effectiveness of a visual merchandise display space would depend on a few key factors:

- The type of merchandise you sell
- The location of the building
- Your store design
- The amount you are willing to allocate to the process

Display space allocation is the most complicated challenge facing most retailers. New products are constantly been introduced into the market. As those new products are brought into the store, the visual merchandiser is charged with the responsibility of finding display space for all of the new products.

One-third of the products each year in an average retail, are new products. Each new product brings with it the accompanying challenge of finding a suitable spot on the shop floor.

To ensure an effective use of your display space, take the following into consideration:

Set a realistic budget

The first thing that needs to be taken into consideration is your budget. How much will you realistically spend on visual merchandising; knowing fully well the benefits of the process?

Answering this question would help you set budgetary priorities to ensure you focus your spending on essential elements such as lighting, display area, fixtures, shelving, storage units and furniture as well as floor and wall coverings.

Create a blueprint

A blueprint of your display space taking into consideration you product line is another point to consider when developing your visual merchandising display plan.

You need to monitor your sales volume, price point and profit margin to ensure that you are effectively using your display space. By monitoring your results, you can keep tweaking your blueprint to ensure you are making maximum use of your display space.

Plan the traffic flow

Customers need to be able to properly examine the products from all angles to make an informed buying decision. Ensure you allow sufficient space for aisles and give consideration to the projected traffic flow.

Remember, you would want your customers to move through your display areas and to the checkout counter with ease. Designing customer flow and accessibility into the visual merchandising display blueprint would help make the process smoother.

There are three basic visual merchandising display space structural frameworks:

Open Structure

An open structure enables customer flow from one product to the next without any barriers or obstacles. The open structure enables the separation of space; however it is done in such a way that it does not hinder the movement of customers around the display.

Grid Structure

In the grid structure, products are displayed in enclosed spaces according to product categories. Adequate segregation is provided on every product category. If the store carries a lot of different product categories extensive efforts are made to ensure each product category is well separated from the next.

Boutique Structure

With the boutique structure, products are placed next to each other. This allows the customer the freedom to choose at will. The drawback of this structure is it can be difficult for the customer to navigate through the products.

In retail; space means money. The store has to be designed in such a way that it optimises the selling area and minimises the non-selling areas.

The selling area is used to present the merchandise and the non-selling section is taken up by passage space, aisles, staircases, lifts, facilities, and the back area. The area mix in a usual department store is: selling area about 65%, circulation area 15% and back area 20%.

In a ready-made garment retail store; setting up the size of the selling space starts with a wardrobe audit where a sample size of the customer section is intercepted and their wardrobe mix of garments and accessories planned out.

This will determine the number of styles and the range width of the same category. Then a store design is made based on the space integration. The selling space is then planned in terms of size and place of merchandise and based on the mix of staple, convenience and impulse merchandise.

How to use space well

The display of a good retail store with attractive windows and an inviting entrance attracts the customer to enter. The customer enters the store and often keeps walking inside following the walkway wherever it leads or sometimes takes a while to look for directions within the store. Sometimes the customer's attention is drawn to certain displays and merchandise presentations before he moves on.

Merchandise can be efficiently displayed on a variety of fixtures such as gondolas, tables, cubes, mannequins, waterfalls and other racks. Display cases and manufacturer point-of-purchase displays are also handy.

A fixture should not only match the merchandise, but also the environment created in the store. Each fixture is presenting the merchandise to the public and as such acts as a silent salesperson.

The space must be specially designed for the type of product being sold in that section. For example, a bookstore requires many shelving units to hold some products that can be arranged by category. On the other hand, a clothing store will need more open spaces to fully display all its merchandise. Once within the store, the customer needs to be guided silently to where he/she wants to go and also expose him/her to the entire store offering. This can be achieved by setting up the flow and the location of the merchandise.

The aisles forming a pattern flow can be of different types based on the store arrangement. The section occupied by the aisles is normally 12-15% of the store carpet area.

Below are some types flow layouts you can choose from:

Free Flow

This layout is used in stores where the merchandise and fixtures are grouped in clusters.

Grid Flow

This type is usually used in supermarkets where the aisles and fixtures are at right angles to each other.

Race Track

This is generally utilized in larger and wider stores where the customer is made to circle around the floor and get back to the beginning, usually the lift or the staircase lobby, to move to the next level of the store.

Herringbone Flow

This is used most of the times for a narrow store of at most 40 ft. wide wherein the freeway is a single two-way one, bisecting the store along its length with "side roads' leading to the walls from it.

The proper utilisation of store space will require the retailer to focus on these three important steps simultaneously:

Step One
Get the appropriate space and product assortment

Retailers optimise and rationalise their assortments based on enhanced analysis of profitability and the apprehension that variety may be overwhelming for customers.

They know they need to do a better job of understanding the assortment. So they assume the role of selector and chief buyer on behalf of the consumers. The positions of various goods are chosen carefully to ensure that the customer is exposed to the entire store; thus increasing the possibility of a purchase.

Step Two
Systematize strategies to manage space

Retailers should re-evaluate their business operations; standardise new and revise older formats. They should competently segment and align their retail space to consumer needs and purchasing behavior.

At the same time they should explore other opportunities for growth.

Step Three
Integrate online and offline channels

The increasing importance of online shopping is changing notions of space management. It introduces the concept of the "endless aisle" and encourages retailers to treat the Internet as an integral part of their operations.

The retail business is very competitive, with thousands of contending retail establishments vying for attention, space management does not end with optimisation.

It creates greater opportunity for merchandise promotion and presentation, which will not only result in higher profit margin but also customers retention.

Below are additional important tips for optimising your store space relative to effective utilization of your fixtures:

Use modern fixtures

An article titled "The Psychology of Shopping," looks at retailing nearly four decades ago. It revealed that the retail giants of the 1970s relied heavily on the philosophy of "pile it high; sell it cheap" and they found success with that philosophy.

Although retailers are currently using more sophisticated ways of capturing the attention of shoppers, this philosophy remains pervasive. To successfully compete in the contemporary retail environment requires you change your philosophy along with your fixtures to more modern eye-catching fixtures.

Choose fixture to match your target market

Pick displays and fixtures that are distinctively suited to your target market.

Who is your target market?

What type of customer do you have?

Take a detailed look at your own store. In what ways are the store fixtures and displays matching the types of customers you wish to attract?

Plan your display strategies

Plan your space using display systems that make it trouble-free for your customers.

The width of the aisles needs to be selected according to the density and traffic pattern.

The main aisle or 'highway' in a department store is six feet wide, which is the width of a double doorway. It facilitates easy passage in both directions. The side aisles or 'side roads' that branch out are three or four feet wide.

In supermarkets, the aisles are three feet wide and form a denser grid around the fixtures.

When planning you display space, you need to take into account the following:

- The average person's field of vision tends to be around 170 degrees
- The number of product categories in the store
- The percentage of space to be allotted to each category
- The volume of merchandise in each category
- The relative placement of each category

How to implement good space allocation

The primary purpose of retail space is to stock and sell product to consumers. The spaces must be designed in a way that promotes an enjoyable and hassle-free shopping experience for the consumer.

The shelf space problem is quite different depending on whether we take the perspective of the manufacturer or the retailer.

Manufacturers want to maximise the sales and profits of their products, and as such always want more and better space to be allocated to their brands.

Retailers want to maximize category sales and profits, regardless of brand identity; they must allocate a fixed amount of shelf space in the best possible way.

Here are a few things to consider when allocating display space:

Fixture arrangement

One of the most common fixtures in stores are gondolas – movable shelving that are accessible from all sides.

They should be lined up in rows as in grocery, hardware and drug stores or used singly to form an island.

When placing racks, progress from small fixtures to large fixtures near the back walls. When working with hard goods, place cubes in the front with gondolas to the rear of the department or store.

Higher end stores require fewer fixtures because there are less merchandise. Use primarily T-stands and four ways to create an illusion of space for selective goods.

This is necessary to sell higher ticket products.

Contextual Merchandising

Similar merchandise should be grouped together on the end-cap and gondola sides. The end-cap should indicate the type of related merchandise on the gondola sides. For example, golf balls displayed on an end-cap should indicate that related golf accessories are located on gondola sides.

End-caps are units at the end of aisles. End-caps are important selling fixtures that should be used for high ticket impulse or seasonal merchandise.

Centralise high ticket products

Customers usually look to the center of gondola sides first before looking either to the left or right. Additional high ticket impulse items should be placed in the center of gondola sides and other related merchandise to either the left or right.

Larger more expensive merchandise should be placed to the right.

Furthermore, high ticket items should be placed at eye level.

Allow contact

If possible, remove a sample from packaging to allow customers to touch and feel the items. Old merchandise should be cleaned and pulled forward as new merchandises are added to the display.

Use a starter gap in which at least one item is missing, so the customer will not feel like they are messing up a neat display.

Create rainbow presentation

Make stimulating displays with mass merchandise by using quantity and color. A good way of arranging merchandise on a gondola is by color. People think of colors in a rainbow pattern and are comfortable with that sort of presentation.

Display merchandise in quantity on quads, round and T-stands; use cubes for folded goods.

Restock the display before it gets down to the last item so customers will not get the impression that something is wrong with the item.

If merchandise are broken the remaining items should be moved to the bottom shelves of the gondola.

Use geometric pattern

A well-planned geometric aisle pattern works best to maximize sales. Place aisle displays in an island rather than wing fixtures.

Fixtures that work well for sale items include tub tables, round racks and rectangular rackslay product. Allow need to be three feet between racks.

Leave fire exit free

The aisle leading directly to the fire exit is considered a major aisle. Do not block the fire exit with fixtures or extraneous materials. Legal requirements for aisle width vary from four to eight feet.

The most common aisle width is six feet. Check your local codes for the your local requirements.

Your goal should be to have enough products of display, not over-crowded fixtures and walls. In addition, clearly delineated product categories. Maximising fixture practice requires fresh eyes and a creative spirit alongside a desire to drive sales.

The new representation for retail success includes not only space utilisation but an integrated approach to space management that will drive traffic, increase sales and profitability.

Retailers should understand the changes in consumer behavior and preferences and align their space management strategies accordingly.

Chapter Seven

The Benefits Planogram Software

More and more retailers as well as manufacturers are now using planogram to create images shelf strips, shelf tags and back tags to help store associates produce prompt and accurate visual merchandising display.

A planogram is a marketing instrument used in retail stores. It is an illustration or drawing that provides details of where a product should be placed on a shelf and how many facing that product should be. It is used by a retail store to increase sales and by suppliers to justify the space allocated of brands and new products.

Retailers employ planograms so they come up with product displays that draw customers' interest and help them to sell more products as a result. The complexity of a planogram may differ by the size of store, the software used to create the planogram and the need of the retailer.

Why is planogram good for visual merchandising?

Figure 19: Planogram makes merchandising display easy

As competition heats up; an increasing number of retailers as well as distributors are becoming more aware of the importance of marketing their products. They are beginning to realise that better marketing leads to improved sales.

Planograms are an accurate way of presenting new ideas for product placement, testing merchandising principles and understanding best possible inventory requirements. It is a schematic of shelve and fixture positioning of products on those shelves or fixtures.

Successful retail space planning and management is an important part of the merchandise planning and execution. A well-designed shopping environment catches the attention of customers, prevents stock outs, enhances inventory productivity, reduces operating costs and most of all boosts the financial performance of the store.

Here are the advantages of utilising planogram for visual merchandising:

Guaranteed product placement

Figure 20: Planogram ensures optimum supply chain efficiency

Accurate store-specific planograms ensure optimum supply chain efficiency that results in higher availability to shoppers, maximum stock turn over and the most efficient use of space.

Improved sales

Targeted store-specific planograms direct maximum in-store compliance, resulting in an accurate understanding of product distribution and eventually increase sales.

Tighter inventory control and reduction of stock outs items

Focused store-specific planograms leads to increased sales and profitability, easier product replenishment, reduction in stock and operational costs and an overall enhancement in bottom line contribution.

Satisfying customers with a better visual appeal

Improves customer satisfaction by making it easier to shop in shelves that are well-organised and reduces the time it takes to arrange stock in the store. Influence customer behaviour for trade-up and impulse buying, which result increased sales.

Effective communication tool for staff

Tailors assortments including product launches and group-specific go-to-market strategies so that you can improve cluster results and meet true local demand and effectively communicate with your staff.

Assigned selling potential to every inch of retail space

Enables better management of inventory by allocating shelf space and facings based on movement, which in turn reduces out-of-stocks; streamlines space and floor planning, so that you can increase your space productivity and optimise your capital investment.

Merchandising Tactics

Figure 21: Planogram Enables better inventory management

Improved merchandising best practices by testing and comparison of cause and effect in like stores; translates merchandising strategy into tactics; so that you can drive consistent store execution of your corporate strategic and assortment decisions.

Planograms will give you a good idea of how a display will look before you physically dress that merchandise on to the shelves in your store. This saves you time and ensures you are not frequently distracting and irritating your customers, by always dressing and re-dressing shelves until you find a product layout that works.

Planograms can be as easy as a photo of a preset section or more thorough with numbered peg holes and shelf notches showing exact position of each item.

Planogram diagrams received by a store may be imprecise or worse nearly impractical to implement because the category size, orientation, or shelving in a particular store may not match the planogram.

In some cases, resetting can be hampered by shelf tags and layouts that rely on shortened names.

Product positioning and enhanced sales are just two important reasons why a retailer should be implementing planograms in their stores. Using a planogram helps a retailer design different product layouts and compare them side by side.

Below are some things to consider when implement planogram in your store:

Quality

Includes shelf heights, merchandise placements and the quantity of facings. Shelf heights depend on the volume of the products and ease of reach for the customers.

Merchandise placement illustrates which shelf and where on that shelf a product should be placed. A facing is a row of products. Thus, if a product has two facings, there are two rows of that product on the shelf.

Importance

The arrangement and number of facings merchandise has will considerably change its sales at the store. It will also change the store's overall performance. It is recommended that the product be placed at eye level and have the maximum amounts of facings.

It is significant for the store to let its most profitable products have the most facings and be located at eye level. And avoid wasting space by placing low ticket slow-moving products with low profit margin in premium locations.

Purpose

The objective of the planogram is to increase sales and offer the most popular product the best spot to attract customers. A store should regularly modify the layout of all of its fixtures.

For example, the design of the children formula section in a super-market will be different every few months depending on what is hot in that period.

The stores use a planogram to make a decision on how the section will look and what merchandise will be most available to the cus-tomer. Besides, with each layout of a planogram, the store will make the fixtures appear more aesthetic to the customer.

Time Schedule

Planograms are typically planned a few weeks in advance of its implementation. A company that specializes in planograms and merchandising will design them using specialized software. Then they will be tested on pilot shelves to ensure they are suitable for the store before deploying it.

How Planogram is used

For a chain of retail stores, planogram guarantees the uniformity of product placement at all locations and wholesalers use the sketches to implement the display of their product. In effect, it gives them the highest sales volume.

Independent retailers use planogram to make the best use of shelf space and improve the look of products. Operating with an efficient planogram is one way to ensure products are replenished and maintained in a way that develops the quality of the display.

A good retailer should understand that the key to increased sales is proper merchandising. A planogram is one of the best merchandising tools for presenting products to the customer.

Listed below are the types of commonly used planogram:

Box with text

The most basic form of planograms utilises box shapes to represent to different goods, with the name of the item typed inside the box.

For example, a planogram intended for a noodle aisle might have rows of larger rectangular boxes to packs of instant noodles.

The brand of instant noodles will be written inside of the box. There may be two rows of each brand depending on the store's requirement.

If the store is usually selling more of one brand, there will be more facings of the high seller. These planograms are typically black and white, two-dimensional diagrams intended for use in grocery stores or areas of retail department stores where merchandise are moving fast.

Pictorial

Pictorial planogram is normally used in clothing and department stores wherein displays are more important and arrangement is essential.

Pictorial planograms are more difficult and thorough compared with the basic planograms.

Pictorial planograms include images of the product and how it should be displayed.

It may show how shirts should be arranged on the shelf or it may demonstrate how dishes or small appliances should be displayed. These planograms are generally flat, two-dimensional, computerised illustrations.

They are typically drawn more precisely to scale and are in color to give an exact representation of how the items are to be displayed.

3-D

Planogram application differs by retail sector. Three-dimensional planograms are usually drawn to scale and include aerial views of the area. As technology advances, so to do the applications and software used to create planograms.

The 3-D type includes whole department layout. Computer generated photographic illustrations of how the department, including promotions and displays should appear. These technologies have led to the growing popularity of three-dimensional planograms.

Fast-moving consumer product industry and supermarkets most of the time use text and box based planograms that optimizes shelf space, inventory turns, and profit margins.

Department Stores are more focused on presentation therefore use pictorial planograms that project "the image" and also identify each product.

Factors to consider when implementing planogram that makes the buying process easier for the customer, which simultaneously result in increased sales for the store are:

Planned Category

Customers might need a product but prior to going to the store have not determined which brand, size, quantity and flavour they require. Having planned category help make customer decision easier.

Impulse buying

A customer might not have plans of buying an item, but seeing the item on display might trigger their desire to buy it.

Substitution

An appropriately merchandised planogram can influence trade-up or trade-down purchases. For example, a customer originally plans to purchase Brand 'A' but proper planogramming directs the customer to Brand 'B' which is offered as a better value.

Triggered

The busy customers frequently appear at the store knowing what they want to purchase; they just don't have a specific list. A "triggered" purchase takes place when they see the product on the shelf which serves as a reminder and that encourages them to buy.

Contextual

Making sure that product category is accurately placed through the aid of correct planogramming will lead to larger transactions and happier consumers.

An incremental purchase is completed as a result of purchasing another product. For example, a customer purchases paint and the appropriately arranged planogram reminds them of the need for a brush, tape, and other items needed to perform the task.

One very essential rule of good quality planogramming is "always anticipating the customer's need." Picture strips and tags are well-liked by shoppers because it helps them understand "product-to-price" identification and let customers know that an item is sold even if it is currently out of stock.

How does planogram work?

The goal is to take full advantage of the quantity of merchandise on display and the amount of sales by arranging merchandise in a way that they will look enticing to customers.

Planogram was designed aim of:

> ➢ Increasing sales
> ➢ Increasing profits
> ➢ Creating a proper way of introducing a new product
> ➢ Supporting a new merchandising approach

Deviating from the planogram defeats the rationale of any of the above stated goals.

The full benefits of planogram can be best achieved if the following steps are being followed:

Step One
Identify the purpose
Decide product positioning and sales betterment are few reasons why you should implement planogram. Outline the kind of display you plan on implementing.

Step Two

Map out the display

The display cases and shelves are the most important elements of a planogram. Start by illustrating the backdrop and draw as accurately as possible so it can be used literally as instructions for organising your shelves.

Step Three

Organize your merchandise

Try out different ways of arranging your merchandise so that they fit as best as possible and will be easily seen.

Decide where you want the products to be positioned using shapes that have the same dimensions and forms of the actual products.

Step Four

Add Labels

Using labels and product images will give you the absolute feel of what you have arranged. It will also let anyone involved in the planning envisage the display.

Step Five

Implement It

Use the illustration to create the life size display. If all of your dimensions are accurate, you should be confident that everything will fit as you planned.

To fully appreciate the value of planogram, any retailer deciding to implement planogram should first be able to read and understand diagrams.

Here are a few pointers to help you read and understand planogram:

Determine whether you have the appropriate planogram for your store. Some retail chains will have different planograms to accommodate the various sizes of stores.

To ensure you are merchandising the right product, match the bar code on the product with your SKU list. This is a listing of all the products and the number of facings, or the number of times each product is to be merchandised on the shelf.

Most planogram software takes some time to master fully, so start with a small display area in your store which contains only a few lines. Locate the lead-in arrow, in the bottom left corner of the schematic. This shows the direction in which the planogram is to be set.

When implementing planogram it is recommended you allocate space based upon product sales performance. A basic rule of planograming is to ensure there are enough products on the shelf to meet the customer's requirement.

Knowing how to read a planogram is a key component of a successful visual merchandising display strategy. It aids in speeding up product placement on the shop floor and increase performance efficiency.

What can you do in your store right now to implement planogram?

Here are some things to consider when implementing planogram:

Location

Where in the store located?

Are there secondary placements?

Category Space Allocation

How much space will be allocated to each category?

Product Space

What will spaces allocation be based upon: sales, movement, mandates or inventory thresholds?

Layout

How will the planogram be structured based upon: price, brand or manufacturers?

Labels/ Signage

How would the category or section benefit from signage or point of purchase materials?

Planogram makes the work of your employees easy at store level as they do not need to do the thinking about where products are to be placed, increasing staff productivity and decreasing shrinkage.

Chapter Eight

How To Profitably Display Merchandise

London based Harrods is one of the most successful retailer in the world. Royalties, A-list stars and the "Who-is-Who" from around the world fly to London just to shop at Harrods.

What is responsible for Harrods spectacular success?

There are three factors responsible for Harrods phenomenon success...

- Good store design
- Attractive visual merchandise display
- Effective loss prevention strategy

The subject of loss prevention is something that has never been taken seriously by the retail industry even though the industry spends billions every year on loss prevention. In the last ten years loss prevention spending has increased tremendously. In 2011 the total cost of retail crime plus loss prevention was $128 billion; but retail shrinkage rose to $119 billion.

So why is it that despite the huge amount spent on loss prevention, retail shrinkage continues to rise?

To answer this question, I will give you a quick tour of Harrods.

Harrods store design and visual merchandising displays are definitely factors in its success. The key factor to Harrods' success though is its ability to remain profitable. Profit is king in retail. In retail the formula for making profit is to increase sales and reduce shrinkage.

Increasing sales requires a good store design and attractive visual merchandising; whereas reducing shrinkage calls for an effective loss prevention strategy.

This is what Harrods and most successful retailers have over the rest of the retail industry: their ability to simultaneously increase sales and reduce shrinkage. Most retailers know how to increase sales, however, when it comes to reducing their shrinkage, they are challenged.

Getting the two right is the fundamental principle of retail success. No retailer can succeed without simultaneously increasing sales and reducing shrinkage.

Why do shrinkage reduction or loss prevention measures fail in most retail organisations?

Loss prevention measures fail in retail is a result of the following reasons:

- Lack of understanding of the subject
- Senior management's failure to prioritise
- Outsourcing loss prevention without a mechanism for accountability
- Inexperienced loss prevention managers
- Ineffective use of loss prevention technology.

Harrods is the first retail store that I have ever entered that has no visible blind spots. I am not saying that there are absolutely no blind spots as I managed to spot a few.

However, the difference with other stores is that they are not visible to the unprofessional eyes.

Anyone deciding to shoplift in Harrods would have to be:

- A professional shoplifter or part of an organised retail crime syndicate
- Really brave
- Really stupid

Products are displayed in such a manner that each department seems wide open. Store staff can stand at one end of a department and have a clear view of the entire department.

Figure 22: Harrods drastically reduced the possibility of shoplifting

There is CCTV in every corner of the store; in addition store assistants buzzing around like bees make it difficult for anyone who might intend to shoplift.

I will not go as far as to say that it is impossible to shoplift at Harrods; because I know shoplifting prevention requires the implementation of a raft of strategies.

However, by designing their store as they have done; by displaying their products in the manner that they do and by taking loss prevention measures seriously; Harrods have drastically reduced the possibility of shoplifting.

Now contrast Harrods loss prevention strategy with a store in the top ten UK retailers that I once worked for as a store detective.

This was a few years back. On my very first day of work, as I was in the middle of a briefing with the officer I was to relieve, I noticed a couple walk into the store and head for the coat section. I stood there perplexed as I witnessed the lady remove one of the coats from the hanger; put it on and then casually walk to the exit with her partner and scurry into the waiting getaway car.

£900 walked out the door with such incredible ease, making me think "Holy cow! How can this sort of thing happen in broad daylight?"

The answer was actually quite apparent: The coats were prominently displayed right close to the exit.

Keeping this experience as a vivid memory, any time I was assigned to a different store, I took great care to walk around and look for high value items that were not securely displayed. I would call the store manager over and advise that the items be relocated to a more secure location within the store. To my disbelief, most managers failed to take my advice – in their eyes, I was merely a store detective. What the heck did I know about visual merchandising?

As a second example: I was working at a store in London Colney; immediately upon entering the store I noticed coats worth £250 prominently displayed near the store entrance.

Without hesitation, I located the store manager and expressed my concern to him. I even joked with him how even the CIA Director at the time, George Tenant, could not possibly protect those coats where they were positioned.

This manager chose to ignore my warning and a few hours later, some of the coats were stolen; just as I had predicted. When I approached the manager again, I figured he would pay more attention to me now that my gloomy prediction came true. Once again, he failed to heed my warning. I finally got his attention but only after 20 of the 25 coats were stolen.

At this same location, there are two big retailers who shared a single toilet facility located outside of both stores. Shoplifters knew this and would steal from one store, head to the direction of the toilet, pass through the other store and escape.

When they were stopped and questioned by our store security, they would always mention they were on their way to the toilet. They were correct about heading in that direction; given the location of the toilet.

The mere location of the toilet caused the stores to lose thousands of pounds to shoplifting. Yet neither store's management could pinpoint the location of the toilet as one of the primary causes for their shrinkage.

I share these stories with you to emphasize a very important point: Shoplifting occurs in most retail stores simply because it is allowed to take place.

Shoplifting is a crime of opportunity; eliminate the opportunity and you reduce its possibility.

Figure 23: To increase sales yet fail to reduce profit draining activities is false economy

To increase sales yet fail to reduce profit draining activities is false economy. Many retailers feel loss prevention is something that they could do if they had the resources.

The reality is: it is something that you cannot afford not to do because no retailer can become profitable without implementing effective loss prevention measures.

Senior management's failure to prioritise

Ninety to 95% of retail loss prevention department managers are ex-service personnel. As a result of their law enforcement background, they take the law enforcement approach to their work. They focus mainly on arresting shoplifters and dishonest employees.

While it is true that shoplifting and employee theft accounts for almost 70% of retail shrinkage, they are not the sole cause of shrinkage. Furthermore, shoplifting and employee dishonesty cannot be tackled by solely arresting individuals.

Preventative measures such as good store design and visual merchandise displays; as I mentioned in the case of Harrods, are required to make any preventative measure effective.

Figure 24: Many retail loss prevention managers know very little about store design and visual merchandising

However, due to the fact that there are still retail loss prevention managers who know very little about store design and visual merchandising; many of them are unable to incorporate these aspects into their loss prevention strategies. As a result most loss prevention measures fail.

Outsourcing loss prevention without a mechanism for accountability

"The average retailer makes a 1% net profit out of each dollar and the average industry shrinkage percentage is 2.6%. This means that shrinkage is almost three times the average retailer's profit margin. By reducing retail shrinkage by 50% – from 2.6 cents to 1.3 cents, a retailer could more than double his profits: from 1 cent to 2.3 cents. (Crosset Company newsletter." June 2010).

Some retailers outsource their loss prevention department to outside contractors. As laudable as this may seem, it is a seriously flawed idea because retailers are sometimes incapable of clearly articulating their expected outcome.

When a job is subcontracted, there is usually an expected outcome. However, if the retailer outsourcing the job cannot articulate their expected outcome, it is difficult to hold the contractor accountable.

Wal-Mart founder Sam Walton once described retail shrinkage as a "profit killer". He was right. High shrinkage is responsible for the death of many retail organisations.

The benefit of a good store design and visual merchandising display is increased sales. So as you develop the plan your store design or visual merchandising display plans, you need to ensure that the safety of the merchandises remain paramount.

In the final analysis you are in business to make profit. And you cannot make profit if you increase sales at the expense of the security of your merchandises.

Without losing the original purpose of your store design and visual merchandising display, you can apply changes to the way in which fixtures are arranged in your store in order to decrease the chances of shoplifting.

One way of doing this is to locate smaller items in places that are visible to employees. Furthermore, positioning employees in key areas of the store is a good strategy to raise the apprehension of shoplifters.

Larger products need to be placed in smaller quantities to prevent the store from appearing cluttered. Poor display of large products can obscure the view of employees and increase the possibility for shoplifting.

Aisles and shelves need to be properly labelled to ensure customers can easily and quickly locate merchandises.

In addition to labelling; installing proper lighting will attract buyers to merchandise as well as allow your employees to observe the surroundings easily.

There is no fool-proof way of preventing shoplifting. However, the installation of security systems such as CCTV and mirrors can reduce incidence of shoplifting in your store. Security mirrors optimize employee's view of the store and reduce blind spots.

How to increase your sales and simultaneously increase your profit?

The following are effective steps for increasing sales and profit with a good store design and merchandising display:

Step 1:
Locate smaller products close to areas that employees frequent to reduce the risk of shoplifting.

Step 2:
Reduce the number of large products on display to allow store employees unhindered views of the store.

Step 3:
Position employees in key areas of the store to increase overall security.

Step 4:
Install security mirrors in the store to reduce blind spots and increase surveillance.

Step 5:

Use CCTV in areas that are not regularly frequented by employees and locate high ticket items under cameras.

Step 6:

Ensure your Loss Prevention Department is involved in the planning of your store design and visual merchandising display.

Years ago, shoplifting was confined to the homeless out for food and drink or drug addicts wishing to feed their habit. Today shoplifting is conducted by retail crime gangs using more sophisticated methods, never before seen in the industry.

Within four minutes, an organised retail crime gang can steal seven thousand pounds worth of products from your store. Think about this the next time you develop your store design and visual merchandising display strategy.

Summary

Since 2007, twenty-four thousand four hundred and forty-six (24, 446) large and medium size retail stores close down resulting in two hundred and nineteen thousand five hundred and two thousand (219,502) retail staff losing their jobs.

These days, one can almost walk around the High Street and take a bet with hundred per cent accuracy on which High Street retailer will be out of business the next week, month or year.

If someone was to place a gun to my head and force me to choose the top five High Street retailers who will cease to exist five years from today, my pick will be the following:

- PC World
- Staples
- WH Smith
- HMV
- Dixons

When they eventually close shop, they will blame the recession and difficult trading conditions.

However, what I have proved in this books is, success or failure in retail has little to do with external factors.

Retailers fail because they do not give thought to the things we have discussed in this book. It is my hope that you immediately put the information you have learnt into action in your business.

I have tried to make the information as practical as possible in order for them to be easily implemented. I have done my part, it is your turn.

Good luck!

Great Books by Romeo

Book Romeo now!

+44(0)78 650 49508

romeo@theprofitexperts.co.uk

27.9% The Most Effective Retail Shrinkage Reduction Technologies

Prior to investing in any technology, there are vital questions that need to answered; those questions along with their answers can be found in this e-book.

This e-book was conceived out of our own desperate efforts to answer those questions.

What you will learn:

- Technologies That Prevent Employee Theft
- Technologies That Prevent Shoplifting

- Receiving Technologies
- Multi-purpose Technologies

12.24% The Most Effective Retail Employee Error Reduction Strategies

Employee errors in pricing, accounting and receiving contribute approximately 18% of retail shrinkage; this equates to £18,623 in losses to an average supermarket or store and almost £49,679 in losses to a superstore. This means that a store or supermarket that operates with a 1% net profit will need to make an additional £3million in annual sales in order to recover profit lost due to employee errors. By the same measure a typical hyper store will need to increase its sales by £8million.

You will learn:

- Constitutes as Retail Employee Error
- to Calculate the Cost of Employee Error
- to Calculate Additional Sales Required to Recover Losses Caused by Employee Error
- of Employee Error
- to Reduce Employee Error
- Ultimate Employee Error Prevention Formula
- to Apply the Lessons from This E-Book to Your Business

43.5% The Most Effective Retail Profit Protection Strategies

The retail landscape is changing rapidly with the constant increase in internet shopping. From 2005 to 2009, the online shopping population grew to 1.6 billion.

It is predicted to rise to 2.3 billion by 2014 with gross revenue totalling $778.6 billion. This is bad news for traditional brick and mortar retail businesses.

The question is: are you prepared? You will find your answer in this eBook.

What you will learn:

- The Conventional Approach to Loss prevention
- Why Loss Prevention is Critical to Retail
- Loss Prevention Spending vs Return on Investment
- What You Are Losing
- Profit vs Sales Calculation
- How to Create a Culture of Loss Prevention
- Effective Shrinkage Management Strategies
- The Ultimate Profit Protection Formula

24.5% The Most Effective Perishable And Non-Perishable Shrinkage Reduction Strategies

This e-book is jam packed with information on the causes of retail shrinkage, types of retail shrinkage, the cost of shrinkage to the retail industry and how shrinkage can be prevented. It is a comprehensive e-book on how and why shrinkage occurs and it provides a step-by-step guide on how to prevent shrinkage.

You will learn:

- An Introduction to Perishable Shrinkage
- Breakdown of Perishable Shrinkage
- Causes of Perishable Shrinkage
- How to Prevent Perishable Shrinkage
- The Ultimate Perishable Shrinkage Prevention Formula
- An Introduction to Non-Perishable Shrinkage
- Classification of Non-Perishable Shrinkage
- Breakdown of Non-Perishable Shrinkage

- Strategies for Preventing Non-Perishable Shrinkage
- The Ultimate Non-Perishable Shrinkage Prevention Formula
- How to Apply The Lessons From This E-Book to Your Business

27.8% The Most Effective Retail Employee Theft Reduction Strategies

The majority of retail employees are decent people who go to work each day to serve their customers and make their living.

However, there are the rotten apples that contaminate the good names of the rest.

This e-book is an instructional guide to retailers to show them how to minimise and prevent employee theft in their stores. Like shoplifting most incidents of employee theft occur because the opportunity exists. When retailers remove the opportunity, they can reduce the possibilities. This e-book will show retailers how to remove the opportunities that allow employee theft in their stores.

You will learn:

- Why Employees Steal
- The Process of Employee Theft
- Signs of Employee Theft
- How to Calculate the Cost of Employee Theft
- How to Prevent Employee Theft
- How Technology Can Help Prevent Employee Theft
- The Ultimate Employee Theft Prevention Formula

84%: The Most Effective Strategies for Increasing Retail Profit

The formula for increasing profit in retail is to increase sales and reduce shrinkage. How can retailers increase sales and reduce shrinkage? The answer is in this book.

You will learn everything you need to know about:

- Creating a Culture of Loss Prevention
- Employee Error
- Employee Theft
- Shoplifting
- Perishable and Non-Perishable Shrinkage
- Receiving Shrinkage
- Technologies that Help to Reduce Retail Shrinkage

Visual Merchandise: How to Create a Beautiful Yet Profitable Display

Merchandise display is the most effective form of advertising for a retail store. The more attractive a display, the higher the possibility of increasing sales. This book will show retailers how to create a display that is so attractive that it would increase their footfall tenfold.

You will learn:

- The psychology behind visual merchandising
- How to use visual merchandising to increase retail sales
- Challenges facing visual merchandisers
- How to burst the price myth with creative merchandise display
- The best merchandise display strategies
- How to maximise display space allocation with creative fixtures
- The pros and cons of using a planogram
- The pros and cons of hiring visual merchandising companies
- Most effective visual merchandise technologies
- How to display merchandise for maximum profit

Store Design Blueprint: How to Design an Attractive But Profitable Store

There are three fundamental principles that underpin a retail store design:

1. Attract customers as they pass by the store
2. Entice them to enter the store
3. Persuade them to buy

The aim of this book is to show retailers how to apply these principles to this store design.

You will learn:

- Store design psychology – what you must know to succeed

- Store design – Image selling

- How to use store design to increase sales

- Store design for increased customer flow

- Choosing your store colour and layout

- The best retail store lighting system

- How to wow customers with creative storefront design

- How to choose the right materials for store design

- Designing store for profit – design security

- Store design technologies

How to Market and Manage A Professional Firm Series: How to make 7 Figure annually as a doctor, dentist, accountant, lawyer, consultant and private security firm owner.

There are four elements essential for the success of any business:

1. Visionary leadership

2. Great people

3. Good system

4. Good marketing system

In the How to Market and Manage A Professional Firm Series, we teach professional entrepreneurs how to effectively utilize these four elements for the development of their businesses.

Many professionals are good technicians. They are good at their professions, however, when it comes to running business they are challenged.

The aim of the 7 Figure Code Books Series is to show professionals how to enhance their technical skills and apply similar levels of structural thinking into building a 7 Figure business.

There is no reason why a doctor or lawyer should not be able to easily make 7 Figure per annum. We show them how to achieve this in the How to Market and Manage A Professional Firm Series.

You will learn:

- How to create an effective business system that runs on auto-pilot
- How to recruit and retain only top talents
- How to develop an effective marketing system
- How to create new market for a product or service
- How the attract new clients and retain existing ones

Book Romeo

Book Romeo now by calling:

+44(0)78 650 49508

Or email: romeo@theprofitexperts.co.uk

Printed in Great Britain
by Amazon